William H. Taft

27th President of the United States

Lucille Falkof

GARRETT EDUCATIONAL CORPORATION

Cover: *Official presidential portrait of William H. Taft by Anders L. Zorn.* (Copyrighted by the White House Historical Association; photograph by the National Geographic Society.)

Manufactured in the United States of America

Edited and produced by Synthegraphics Corporation

Library of Congress Cataloging in Publication Data

Falkof, Lucille, 1924–
  William H. Taft, 27th president of the United States / Lucille Falkof.
       p.   cm. – (Presidents of the United States)
   Includes bibliographical references.
   Summary: Presents the life of William H. Taft, including his childhood, education, employment, and political career.
   1. Taft, William H. (William Howard), 1857–1930 – Juvenile literature.   2. Presidents – United States – Biography – Juvenile literature.   3. United States – Politics and government – 1909–1913 – Juvenile literature.   [1. Taft, William H. (William Howard), 1857–1930.   2. Presidents.]   I. Title.   II. Title: William H. Taft, twenty-seventh president of the United States.   III. Series.
E762.F35   1990   973.91′2′092 – dc20
[B]   [92]   89-39947
ISBN 0-944483-56-9   CIP
                                                          AC

Contents

Chronology for
William H. Taft

1857   Born on September 15

1874–   Attended Yale University
1878

1880   Graduated from Cincinnati Law School; admitted to the Ohio bar

1881   Received first political appointment as assistant county prosecutor

1886   Married Helen (Nellie) Herron on June 19

1887   Appointed judge of the Ohio Superior Court

1890   Appointed solicitor general in President Benjamin Harrison's administration

1892   Appointed federal circuit judge of the Sixth Circuit Court of Appeals

1900–   Headed Philippine Commission and served
1903   as first U.S. governor of the Philippines

1904   Appointed secretary of war in President Theodore Roosevelt's administration

1909–   Served as 27th President of the United
1913   States

1913–   Professor of Law at Yale University
1921

1921–   Served as Chief Justice of the United
1930   States Supreme Court

1930   Died on March 8

Chapter 1

The Murder Case that Launched a Career

It was a murder that gave a rising young lawyer, William Howard Taft, the opportunity to star in a court case that would be his first step on a road to the presidency of the United States. The incident ended in a much-publicized trial and a riot.

The murder victim was William Kirk, owner of a livery stable in Cincinnati, Ohio. Charged with the crime were two stable boys, William Berner and Joseph Palmer, who allegedly robbed and murdered their employer on Christmas Eve in 1883. Both boys confessed to the crime, but each argued that he had been led on by the other. Berner was tried first; his lawyer was Tom Campbell. Many local lawyers despised Campbell, a man who seemed to use questionable means to free his clients.

Because Cincinnati had been having a crime wave, the local newspapers headlined the murder trial for weeks. Finally, the jury found Berner guilty only of manslaughter, *not* of murder, despite the fact that he had confessed to the crime and had admitted on the witness stand that he had been at the scene. The citizens were enraged. As the jurors were leaving the courthouse, they were greeted with hisses and calls of "Hang him!"

RIOTING IN THE STREETS

Four days after the verdict, a mass meeting was held. At 10 P.M., a mob of angry citizens approached the jail where Berner was being held and began throwing bricks at the windows. Though the police tried to stop the riot, the fighting went on all night. The mob wanted vengeance, not only on Berner, but also on the lawyer who had saved him from the gallows, Tom Campbell.

The next night, fighting broke out again. This time, however, police prevented the mob from reaching the jailhouse. The angry citizens then stormed the nearby Hamilton County Courthouse and set it on fire. By morning the courthouse had burned to the ground. More than 100 men were wounded and 45 killed in the riot.

Prosecuting a Lawyer

In the spring of 1884, Tom Campbell was brought to trial on charges of bribing jurors in the Berner case. William Taft was part of a small group of lawyers interested in maintaining high standards for the legal profession. He had opposed the shrewd Campbell several times in court and found him suspiciously unethical. Taft, like many of his colleagues, hoped that Campbell would be found guilty. But Campbell was freed when the jurors failed to agree on a verdict.

Learning that Campbell was going to be brought to trial to be disbarred, Taft was eager to help in gathering the necessary evidence to expel Campbell from the law profession. If the trial succeeded, Campbell would never be able to practice law again. The charges against Campbell were that he had obtained jurors "in a corrupt manner" and had been "improperly influencing their verdicts."

The 28-year-old Taft was not unknown in Ohio political circles. Earlier in 1884 he had gone to Columbus, the state capital, to argue for improving the state's criminal law code. He had campaigned for the Republican Party, and his father had been attorney general under President Ulysses S. Grant. So when Taft volunteered his services to investigate the Campbell case, the two senior lawyers on the case, E. W. Kittredge and William M. Ramsey, were happy to accept his offer. Taft, who received no salary for his work, then spent several months traveling throughout Ohio collecting evidence against Campbell.

On January 5, 1885, Ramsey was due to give the final summation for the prosecution to the jury. It was Taft's lucky day, for when Ramsey became ill, he asked Taft to take over. William thereupon delivered a four-hour speech, describing in endless detail every incident in the case. All his life, Taft would deal with problems, legal or otherwise, with gentle logic and reason. The theatrical and emotional delivery of some lawyers just was not his style.

It was, however, Thomas Campbell's style. When he rose two days later to speak in his own defense, the jurors had to be impressed with his flowing hair and elegant beard. They also had to be touched by Campbell's emotional sobs as he spoke, portraying himself as a defender of the poor and the oppressed.

After deliberating at great length, the jury cleared Campbell of the charges. Though Taft may have been disappointed by the results, the people and the lawyers of Cincinnati were impressed with the work he had done. The case added much to the young lawyer's reputation. He was acclaimed a champion of "the forces of decency." However, William Taft had little time to think about being disappointed because he had other things on his mind. He was trying to work up courage to ask a young woman, Nellie Herron, to be his bride.

THE CHERUB OF CINCINNATI

Some saw the new baby at the Alphonse Taft home as looking just like a cherub, so round and plump, with a dimple in one cheek. But by seven weeks, he was so enormous that his mother wrote, "He has such a large waist, that he cannot wear any of the dresses that are made with belts." Being fat was a problem William Taft would have to deal with all of his life. The fact that he was generally good-natured and enjoyed a hearty laugh helped, even though the jokes often were at his expense.

Justice Brew of the U.S. Supreme Court once commented, "Taft is the politest man in Washington—the other day he gave up his seat in a street car to three ladies." This was not as exaggerated as it seemed, for the grown man, at five feet ten inches, at times weighed as much as 340 pounds.

William Howard Taft was fortunate to have been born into a loving and caring family which could trace its ancestry back to the arrival of the first Robert Taft in Braintree, Massachusetts, in 1678. There was an independent streak in the family combined with a touch of wanderlust. William's grandfather, Peter Taft, who came to live with the family in Cincinnati, would thrill young William with stories of how he drove the family cow as his family walked 80 miles one snowy winter from Massachusetts to settle in Vermont. There was also a drive for education. Grandpa Peter was largely self-educated and became a lawyer, a career that William's father, Alphonse, would later follow. It was a family that would not amass any great wealth, but would earn a reputation for honesty and integrity.

William Howard Taft was born in this home in Cincinnati, Ohio, on September 15, 1857. The family eventually included two half-brothers, a sister, and two brothers. (Library of Congress.)

Alphonse and Louise Taft

Though born on a farm in Vermont, Alphonse Taft did not want to be a farmer. Like his father, Alphonse also aspired to be a lawyer, and went on to get his law degree after finishing Yale College in 1833. He then moved from Vermont to Cincinnati to establish a law practice. He selected Cincin-

nati because it was a middle-class town where there were relatively few lawyers.

Following the death of his first wife, Alphonse married
Louise Torrey, who was living in Massachusetts at the time.
Upon her arrival in Cincinnati, Louise found that the Taft
household was already a full one. In addition to two sons from
Alphonse's first marriage—ten-year-old Charles and seven-
year-old Peter—there were Alphonse's parents. They had come
to Cincinnati to help care for the two boys after Alphonse's
first wife died.

But Louise proved equal to the task. She found the elder Tafts kind and helpful, and Louise turned out to be a fine
mother to her two stepsons. And after losing her own first
child to whooping cough, she produced the pride of both
Alphonse's and her life—William Howard Taft, born on September 15, 1857.

Though Alphonse and Louise hoped to have a daughter, two more sons were added to the family. When the fifth
son arrived on December 28, 1861, even William commented
gloomily to his father, "Old Santa Claus brought Horace here
because nobody else wanted him." Finally, a daughter, Frances
Louise, was born in 1865, completing and delighting the
family.

MEETING FATHER'S EXPECTATIONS

On the surface, Alphonse seemed to be a strict and demanding father, believing, he said, that the use of the rod might
be necessary at times. But his sons never remember being
punished that way. In fact, their father's stern manner hid a
gentle and loving man. In a letter to his wife when the chil-

dren were away for the summer with her, he wrote, "There is no noise and no mischief. . .and on the whole it is not satisfactory to have no mischief about the house."

The three sons born to Alphonse and Louise always considered Charles and Peter as brothers, not half-brothers. Being the tallest and heaviest, Will, called "Big Lub" by his brothers, was the leader. Until almost the end of his high school years, Will played baseball enthusiastically. He also loved swimming in an old canal (now one of Cincinnati's main streets) and ice skating on the frozen canal during the winter months.

Because Alphonse Taft had strong feelings about the value of a public education, all the boys were sent to public schools. Will was a popular and bright student, with a fine ability to concentrate even amid the bustle and noise of the household. It was just as well, for Alphonse expected high achievement from his children. He was intolerant of stupidity and laziness. When Willie was 12 years old, his father could not help reporting with pride the achievements of his sons: "Willie and Horace won medals. . .Willie took the first in his class handsomely. His average was 95 and the nearest to him averaged 85. . .I am delighted with his writing and his expression of his thoughts."

Willie could almost have been considered too perfect, if his good nature had not prevented him from taking himself and his achievements too seriously. He even enjoyed the dancing classes run by two white-haired ladies in town. In fact, he was to be an excellent dancer all his life. Even when he was extremely heavy, he proved to be light on his feet.

Nothing seemed to mar the serenity at the Taft home, despite the fact that the Civil War broke out when Will was four years old. Charles Taft, who was almost 18 at the time, could have enlisted, but he chose to continue his studies at Yale. Cincinnati was on the Ohio River and was one of the gateways to the South. The city depended upon southern trade and was sympathetic to the southern cause, but the war did not affect the Taft family.

A Believer in Women's Rights

On November 4, 1908, the day following his election to the presidency, William Howard Taft took time out to attend the laying of the cornerstone of the new Woodward High School in Cincinnati. His deep affection for the school he had attended so many years before was reflected in the words he spoke that day. Woodward was one of the first public high schools in the country to offer a solid preparation for college. Years after his graduation, Taft would serve as president of its alumni association.

While at Woodward, Taft began to enjoy the company of young women. He liked intelligent women, especially if they were also good-looking. It was at Woodward that he wrote an essay on women's suffrage (the right to vote) which revealed his strong belief in women's rights:

> Coeducation...shows clearly that there is no mental inferiority on the part of girls... Give the woman the ballot, and you will make her more important in the eyes of the world. This will strengthen her character... Every woman would then be given an opportunity to earn a livelihood. She would suffer no decrease in compensation for her labor on account of her sex.

Will Taft must have meant these words for he later married a young woman who would match in strength and character the description in his essay.

After his graduation from Woodward High School in the spring of 1874, Will was ready for college. Continuing what had become a family tradition, he enrolled at Yale in the fall.

Chapter 2

For Yale, the Law, and the Republican Party

A lphonse Taft passed on to his sons a dedication to three institutions: Yale, the law, and the Republican Party. For Will Taft, all three were part of his youth, for his father was a Yale man, a lawyer, and a lifetime Republican. With one brief exception during his undergraduate days at Yale, the labels could also be applied to Will.

His casual acceptance of Republicanism was shaken briefly when Will fell under the spell of Professor William Graham Sumner at Yale. Sumner was an advocate for free trade between nations. Unlike the Republicans, he believed that high taxes on imported goods (protectionism) did not really "protect" American industry. He also believed that such taxes increased the cost of living. His lectures on the subject probably influenced Taft later to seek only the most necessary taxes on imported goods.

A CLASS HERO

Alphonse Taft expected his sons to excel in their studies. Eldest brother Charles had won honors at Yale and the next brother, Peter, had the top grades in his class, setting high standards for Will to follow. Alphonse also expected his sons to keep daily accounts of their expenses; he would not tolerate any extravagances. Moreover, he found sports such as baseball and football frivolous "wastes of time." It was a shame because Will would have loved to play both. He certainly had the size for it.

However, Will did have his shining moments as an athlete during his freshman year. The big annual event for freshmen was an old Yale tradition called the "rush." It was a free-for-all mud-wrestling event between the freshmen and the sophomores. In 1874, the Yale faculty was urging that the yearly brawl be stopped. The smaller and lighter freshmen, who usually bore the brunt of the match, were more than willing to forego the rush, but Will thought otherwise.

"Is the glorious freshman class of 1878 to be the first to run away from the wicked sophomores?" he asked. Will's arguments won his classmates over, and he did more than his share at the time of the big event. He barreled his way through the muck to make many a sophomore regret he had come upon the big, burly freshman. Will also won applause from his classmates when he was selected by them to take on the sophomore wrestling champion, whom he promptly pinned to the mat.

College Honors

In his junior year, Will was awarded several honors: one was the math prize; the other, election as class orator. Despite being elected class orator, Taft was not a particularly inspiring speaker. He prepared his speeches well – often too well – giving his listeners more details than they wanted to hear. He also lacked the ability to speak casually in relaxed, off-the-cuff situations. Even at college, he tended to speak too much like a judge in court.

Will graduated second in a class of 132 and was tapped for Yale's famed senior honor society, Skull and Bones. Election to the society was based not only on athletic prowess and intellect, but also on what a student had contributed to undergraduate life at the school. Taft was well qualified for the honor.

FOLLOWING IN THE FAMILY'S FOOTSTEPS

Considering that his father had received his law degree from Yale and that two brothers had received theirs from Columbia University in New York City, it was a bit surprising when Will decided to stay in Cincinnati to attend law school near home. After the hard work he had put in at Yale, law school offered a far more relaxed atmosphere. It consisted mostly of two hours of philosophical discussion, sometimes in the morning and sometimes in the afternoon or early evening.

Will began his studies the summer after graduation from Yale in 1878 by working in his father's law office. The heat, which would always affect Will, slowed his pace and did not encourage much serious study that summer. In the fall, with the short hours of law school, he decided to do what most students at Cincinnati Law School did. To earn money, he took a job as a court reporter for the Cincinnati *Commercial*. That gave Will an excellent opportunity to observe the courts and to see how well or how poorly the wheels of justice turned.

Father Makes the National Scene

As one of the elder statesmen of the Republican Party, Alphonse Taft was asked to run for governor of Ohio in 1875, when the incumbent (currently serving) governor, Rutherford B. Hayes, announced he would not run for a third term. Alphonse agreed, and Will became one of several men who canvassed Cincinnati to get delegates who would support his father at the state convention. But at the convention, Hayes *was* nominated and accepted the nomination. Ever the gentleman and with an eye on party unity, Alphonse Taft withdrew his candidacy in order to make Hayes' nomination unanimous. A year later, Will's father had another opportunity in politics.

The administration of President Ulysses S. Grant was suffering from a series of scandals. When Grant was forced to replace Secretary of War William Belknap, he sought someone whose reputation for honesty was unquestionable. The name of Alphonse Taft was mentioned often, and Grant appointed him to that position in his Cabinet. Three months later, when there was another Cabinet shake-up, Alphonse became attorney general, a position more suited to his legal training and expertise. Through his father's experiences, Will gained his first insight into Washington politics and the workings of the President and his Cabinet.

A Political Plum

Will was taking both his job and his law studies rather casually. His parents were a bit dismayed by Will's attitude toward his work and his studies. They were concerned that he was much too interested in the social scene in Cincinnati. The city had grown in size as well as culture since Alphonse had settled there. Will and his friends took advantage of the entertainment offered by such attractions as a theater, an opera house, and a music hall. He was not too busy to appreciate the charms of the local ladies. Will's opinion was, "Nowhere... will you find girls as pretty, interesting, as stylish, and as fresh."

After graduating from Cincinnati Law School, it was

time for Will to take the Ohio bar examination. In May 1880, he went to Columbus, took the examination, and passed with flying colors, despite the fact that he had spent the evening before the exam with friends, drinking beer and singing Yale songs.

Will might have gone into private practice as a lawyer. His father no longer had a law practice, devoting himself instead to politics, but his brother, Charles, had opened an office. Although Will had the connections and was popular enough to open his own office, he tended to let time and circumstances make decisions for him. Rarely did he take the initiative to strike out on his own. As would happen many more times in his life, he found himself at the right place at the right time.

Will's work as a court reporter brought him into close contact with Miller Outcault, the assistant prosecuting attorney of Hamilton County. It was at the local court that Will had his first experiences with the man he would meet again at the Berner murder trial and who would become his sworn enemy—Tom Campbell. Outcault was convinced that County Prosecutor Sam Drew was plotting with Campbell to try to win the acquittal of a Democratic auditor accused of embezzlement.

Will wrote a series of articles for his newspaper, taking great care to describe Campbell's character and methods, which turned out to be of great help to Outcault. As would happen later in the Berner case, Outcault was not able to prove that Campbell and Drew had tampered with the jury. Drew left office shortly after, and Outcault was elected county prosecutor. He promptly named Will as his assistant.

For the next year, Taft added practical knowledge to his law school training. He prosecuted a series of swindlers, petty thieves, and murderers, which enabled him to acquire confidence in his knowledge of trial and courtroom procedure.

THE REALITY OF POLITICS

In later years, Taft was asked by famed editor William Allen White, "Will you tell me frankly where you get your political pull?" In a most candid manner, Taft replied, "I always had my plate right side up when offices were falling. . . . I got my political pull first through father's prominence, then through the fact that I was hail-fellow-well-met [friendly comrade] with all the political people of the city convention-going type. I also worked hard in my ward."

Despite the fact that Taft, on occasion, attacked men such as Ohio's Republican Party boss, George B. Cox, he managed to stay on speaking terms with them. Taft had the unique ability to strike out against a man's methods of conducting politics without attacking the man personally. Will was apt to forgive some irregularities on the part of party members, but he would never commit such activities himself.

His desire to do what was right probably accounts for Will's brief term as Collector of Internal Revenue for one of the largest districts in the country, covering Ohio and Kentucky. The job offer came from President Chester A. Arthur, who had recently named Alphonse Taft as American minister to the court of the Emperor Franz Joseph, in Vienna, Austro-Hungary.

At age 24, Will was the youngest revenue collector in the country, in an area with a large number of whiskey distilleries. In writing about the appointment, the editor of the liquor industry's journal described Taft as having "the build of a Hercules and the sunny disposition of an innocent child." Taft was soon to lose his innocence.

Resignation

It did not take long for Will to discover why he had been placed in the job. The position of revenue collector was a boring one, consisting mainly of keeping accounts and doing audits. Like most government agencies at the time, the internal revenue agency was filled with northern Civil War veterans. These men had gotten their jobs through patronage, the system of granting political appointments to repay political favors. The appointees did little but collect their salaries; the real work was done by a few trusted employees.

Before long, an Ohio Republican congressman seeking re-election asked Taft to fire some of his most capable men and replace them with people more favorable to the congressman's candidacy. The congressman, Thomas Young, invoked the name of President Arthur in making his demand: "He thinks you are shrewd enough and have sufficient knowledge of Hamilton County to know who these men are. . . He depends upon you as a friend." Will was torn. He was a loyal Republican but he could not, in all fairness, meet Young's demands. Yet he worried that not doing so might undermine or affect his father's position abroad.

In a letter to his father, Will explained the situation and closed with, "I would much rather resign and let someone else do Tom Young's service and dirty work." His father understood Will's position and advised him to handle the situation so it would not offend anyone, if possible. Shortly after, Will personally called upon President Arthur, explained that he wished to go back into private practice, and agreed to stay on for three more months, until a replacement could be found. Relieved of the burden, Will decided to plunge into law full-time and formed a partnership with an old friend of his father's, Major Harlan Page Lloyd.

Not Quite Through

Will, however, was not yet finished with politics. In 1884 his father urged him to work for the election of the Republican candidate for President, James G. Blaine. Though not enthusiastic about Blaine, Will agreed and was soon appointed chief supervisor of elections. His task was to prevent fraud at the polls, an almost impossible assignment in view of the way politics were then conducted in Cincinnati. Will settled for trying to prevent Democratic fraud, a difficult job, for the local police were controlled by the Democratic Party.

The election ended in bloodshed, with a black man slain by a federal marshall for no apparent reason. The U.S. House of Representatives, heavily controlled by Democrats, sent a committee to investigate the election. The United States marshall was found guilty of the crime, and Taft, who was a witness at the hearing, had to admit that his deputies had been totally ineffective.

Chapter 3

The Liberated Lady and the Judge

For a Victorian lady living in the 1880s, Nellie Herron could certainly be considered a "liberated woman." She taught school when young ladies of her upper-middle-class position did little but volunteer work, and she organized a "salon" to discuss literature and the burning issues of the day. Nellie made no attempt to hide her above-average intelligence, and though women would not have the right to vote for almost 40 more years, she did not hesitate to speak her mind. She even dared to go without a male escort to a saloon to drink beer. It took the amiable Mr. Taft five years to woo and win her.

It was not as if Will lacked female companionship as a young man about town. Nor did he hesitate to participate in those community activities that offered amusement, including performing with a local amateur theater group. In fact, he earned quite a reputation for his playing the title role in a mock version of *Sleeping Beauty*. His hilarious protrait of the beautiful maiden so convulsed the audience with laughter that the girls of Cincinnati changed his nickname from "Big Lub" to "Angel."

THE WOOING OF NELLIE HERRON

The Herron and the Taft families moved in the same social circle, and the two fathers were both lawyers and friends. Yet, Helen Herron (always called Nellie), and Will Taft did not meet until a sledding party one winter's night when Nellie was 18 years old. Even then, young Will did not pursue Nellie, and it was probably just as well, for Nellie had very definite ideas about what she expected of marriage. In her diary, she questioned why a man could not enjoy a friendship with a woman in which both could realize "each other's defects and a proper appreciation of their good points without that fatal idealization which is. . .so contemptible. . . . From my point of view, a love which is worthy of the name should always have a beginning in the other [friendship]."

Certainly Will's courtship met Nellie's expectations. Though he took her to a reception at his brother Charlie's home in February 1880, their friendship did not blossom until Taft became a member of Nellie's salon, which met weekly at the Herron home.

Hopelessly in Love

By the winter of 1884, Taft was seeing Nellie regularly, but he was so involved with the Campbell disbarment case that it was not until April 1885 that he proposed. Two events that winter probably gave him the courage to speak up. One was the many accolades (words of praise) he had received for his roll in the Campbell case. The other was that he was offered a job as assistant county solicitor with a yearly salary of $2,500. As was customary at the time, Nellie rejected his proposal two or three times. By now, however, Will was hopelessly in love.

Will's letters to Nellie were passionate and dramatic. "Do not coldly reason away every vestige of feeling you may have for me.... I have walked the streets this morning with the hope of seeing you and with little other excuse." While involved in the Campbell case, he worried that his political life might cause her some suffering. "I hated to think of your linking your fortune with one who has... called down on his head the bitter enmity of such a devilish and powerful combination as that headed by Campbell."

A month after Will first proposed, their engagement was made official. Nellie's mother decided to take her family to a resort in the Adirondack Mountains in New York, the scene of Mrs. Herron's childhood. Will wrote his father that he would stay in Cincinnati to save money. But when Nellie wrote, complaining about the limited menu at the place where the Herron clan was staying, Will found the perfect excuse for visiting his bride-to-be. He went to one of the fanciest grocers in town, selected a trunk-size box, and filled it with every imaginable delicacy. Arriving with the goodies, he was enthusiastically greeted by Nellie and her family. Despite his good intentions to work hard that summer, he found Nellie irresistible, and they spent several wonderful weeks together at the resort.

Frugal Nellie

The wedding was scheduled for June 1886. That spring Nellie and Will were kept busy preparing for the event. The bride's father gave them a lot in Walnut Hills, and Will's father loaned him $6,000 to build a house. Will found his future wife to be a careful manager of their money. She even found a very reasonable boat passage for their honeymoon, and they managed a trip abroad on five dollars a day.

Shortly before their marriage, Nellie went to Washington, D.C. It was her second visit; she had been there once before as a guest at the White House when her father's friend, Rutherford B. Hayes, had been President. During her trip to Washington, Nellie received a letter from Will, teasing her about her frugal ways: "I wonder, Nellie dear, if you and I will ever be there [in Washington] in any official capacity? Oh yes, I forgot; of course we shall when you become secretary of the treasury."

Nellie Herron Taft would prove to be a loving wife, with great ambitions for her husband. She did not hesitate to use praise—and criticism—to spur him on. In choosing Nellie, Will Taft found a strong partner, one who had an astute understanding of politics. He would always be an adoring husband, and Nellie would become his dearest friend and closest advisor.

PLAYING POLITICS

William Taft never trusted Joseph Benson Foraker, an Ohio politician. When Tom Campbell had been tried for bribing a juror, Foraker had been Campbell's defense lawyer. In their private law practices, Taft and Foraker, on opposing sides, had almost come to blows. In a letter to Nellie, Taft called Foraker "a double-faced Campbell man, and when a man bears such a brand, I'll have none of it." Will Taft would soon have to swallow his words.

In 1885 Foraker allied himself with George Cox. They succeeded in building a state political machine strong enough to get Foraker elected governor. In 1887, shortly after Foraker again won the governorship, Will casually asked Nellie, "What would you think if I should be appointed a judge on the state superior court?" Nellie laughed and retorted, "Oh, don't try to be funny. That's perfectly impossible."

But it was possible. The post was an elective one, but the law gave the governor the right to make such an appointment if a vacancy occurred within 30 days of the election. Such a vacancy existed, and Foraker offered the post to Taft. Will accepted the offer and had no trouble winning the election on his own in 1888. Since there was no love lost between the two men, why did Foraker make the offer and why did Taft accept?

For a man who played the political game as well as Foraker, the appointment of Taft was obvious. The governor could claim that he believed court appointments should be nonpartisan—above politics. Foraker also recognized the power of the Taft name as well as Will's intelligence and personality. If the young man was destined to go far in politics, Foraker, who aspired to be President, wanted Taft on his side. As for Will, the idea of gaining such an appointment was too enticing to refuse.

A Year of Change

Many currents of change were stirring in the nation in 1887, the year Taft began his judicial career. The social, economic, and labor problems that Taft would face as judge and later as President were already developing.

Farmers in the Midwest were having difficulty paying their mortgages. Laborers looked at the huge profits being made by the railroads as well as by the oil and coal industries and sought to get "a piece of the pie." They were enraged to find their congressmen overly sympathetic to the corporate millionaires, so labor began to organize in order to get their fair share of the profits. At the same time, respectable middle-class people worried about labor strikes and other activities of radical labor leaders.

The working class was beginning to find its leaders in such men as Robert M. La Follette, a liberal Republican from Wisconsin; Samuel Gompers, who would become president of the American Federation of Labor; and William Jennings Bryan, the Democratic candidate who would oppose Taft for the presidency in 1908. Though Taft was not antilabor, many of his carefully reasoned decisions on the bench would appear to be in opposition to the workingman.

ON THE NATIONAL SCENE

Taft was neither conceited nor overly impressed in regard to his own talents. In general, he tended to be rather modest and was often insecure. Yet he did not hesitate to seek higher office or to pull strings when needed to attain any position. His true lifetime goal was the U.S. Supreme Court, and after only two years on the high court of Ohio, he was already looking to Washington, D.C., to the highest court in the land. His chief advocate turned out to be Foraker, who was now running for his third term as governor of Ohio.

When a vacancy on the Supreme Court arose in 1890, Foraker sent a letter of recommendation for Taft to President Benjamin Harrison, but the President was not about to make such an appointment to satisfy Ohio Republicans. However, he did offer Taft, as a consolation prize, the position of solicitor general. The role was that of general counsel, responsible for drafting legal opinions for the attorney general and members of the President's Cabinet. It also meant that Taft would argue most of the government's cases before the Supreme Court. For Will, this was a first step to being *on* the court, and he looked forward to his new position. For Nellie, who had found the world of the Ohio Superior Court a boring one, it meant a move to the nation's capital and new and interesting people.

Taft's arrival in Washington was hardly an auspicious (notable and promising) beginning. The berth of the railroad car was not constructed for such a large man as William Taft. After enduring a restless night, he arrived in Washington at 6:00 A.M. on a cold, gray morning. There was no one at the station to greet him, no porter to carry his luggage, and he was forced to eat a lonely breakfast at his hotel. Nellie had stayed behind with their six-month-old son, Robert, until Will could find appropriate accommodations for them.

After introducing himself to the attorney general, W. H. Miller, Taft faced further disappointment. His office turned out to be a single shabby room, located up three flights of stairs. His stenographer was a telegraph operator whose services Will could obtain by bellowing for the operator when the wires were quiet.

Washington Social Life

Life improved with the arrival of Nellie and little Robert. The small house at 5 DuPont Circle was difficult to maintain on Taft's $7,000 annual salary, but his half-brother, Charles, advanced the necessary funds. Charles Taft, who had inherited a large sum of money from his maternal grandfather, was always very proud of Will. He would generously help Will out, not only with living expenses, but with campaign expenses as well when Taft needed them later on.

In 1890, Washington society was much simpler than it is today. It consisted of a few "best families," the diplomatic corps, representatives of foreign nations, and top government officials. Dinner parties were small—no more than 12 guests. Occasionally, there were large receptions, but in general, the nation's capital was still considered a cultural outpost by sophisticated European visitors.

There was, however, a group of intelligent and amusing

people whose paths would cross and influence Taft's life. The group included Theodore Roosevelt, a member of the Civil Service Commission; John Hay, Lincoln's secretary, who later became secretary of state; and Senator Henry Cabot Lodge of Massachusetts. Roosevelt already had quite a reputation as a crusader for a number of causes. Both Taft and Roosevelt were about the same age, and though opposite in personality in many ways, they shared a sense of humor and took a liking to one another.

Taft's brief encounters with President Benjamin Harrison gave him his first impressions of what a President should *not* be. "The President is not popular with the members of either house. His manner of treating them is not at all fortunate, and when they have an interview with him, they generally come away mad."

Nellie could boast about a dance they attended where, as Will described it, "all the swells," including the British, Turkish, and Danish ministers, were present. On the whole, however, Washington's social life was not as interesting as Nellie would have liked it, but Will was enjoying the variety of experiences in his work.

The death of his father in 1891 affected Will deeply. Despite the distance between them because of their careers, they had always kept in close touch through letters. Will had visited his father in California, where he had gone for his health. There, even as he was dying, Alphonse envisioned greatness for his son. His father predicted that the presidency would someday be offered to Will, and Alphonse whispered confidently, "There will be no special trouble in your being prepared for it."

But Will was not quite ready to remain in Washington and push himself further into local political circles. He needed a safer harbor for a few years, and a new act of Congress provided the chance.

A Silk Robe for the Judge

The number of cases being brought before federal courts had increased so much that Congress created an appeals court in each of the nation's nine federal circuits in order to improve the way cases moved through the legal system. As soon as word of the new federal appeals court was announced, Taft tapped every connection he had in order to gain an appointment. In March 1892, he was appointed federal circuit judge of the Sixth Circuit Court of Appeals. He held court in three Ohio cities, Cincinnati, Cleveland, and Toledo, as well as in Detroit, Michigan, and Nashville, Tennessee. Will Taft loved the work, and for the first time he ordered a silk judicial robe for himself. Members of the Ohio Superior Court had not worn this ornament of office. The job, however, was arduous and required his being away frequently from Nellie, Robert, and little Helen, born in 1891.

CLASHING WITH LABOR

Both as a superior court judge in Ohio and as a federal judge, Taft was much involved in the development of labor law. The 1890s witnessed an expansion of labor unions. In their efforts to gain some of the profits being made in industry, workers were using such methods as strikes and boycotts. In general, Taft agreed with labor's right to strike (to refuse to work in order to obtain better wages). However, he did not feel the same about the use of boycotts, a request by strikers not to use the goods or services of their employer. The Pullman Company strike in Chicago focused the nation's attention on the growing labor problems, and Taft found himself in the center of the battle.

The Pullman Strike

George Pullman was the inventor and manufacturer of the first sleeping cars for the railroads. His company was looked upon as a model corporation, based on the employer's fatherly concern for his employees. Outside of Chicago, Pullman had created a town close to the plant, with well-planned streets, rental homes for the workers, public services, and company stores. The Pullman Company was hailed as a model of the future.

The workers, however, knew otherwise. They paid 10 percent more for city water and gas, and despite huge profits the year before, in 1894, Pullman cut wages 25 percent and began laying off workers. But he did not reduce rents and other charges to employees. In protest, the workers went on strike, refusing to work until their demands were met. When Pullman refused to negotiate a wage increase or a rent decrease, the workers called in the head of the American Railway Union, a gentle, sad-faced individual named Eugene Debs. Debs called for a nationwide boycott, demanding that workers everywhere refuse to handle any railroad car produced by the Pullman Company.

Though Taft believed labor had the right to strike, he was furious when the Pullman boycott paralyzed the nation by halting the shipment of food, goods, and even the United States mail. The boycott resulted in rioting and bloodshed. His position as a federal judge prevented Taft from any public utterance on the subject, but in his personal correspondence he expressed his opinion strongly. "It is the most outrageous strike in the history of this country and ought to fail miserably. . . . The workingmen seem to be in the hands of the most demagogic [using false claims and promises to gain power] and insane leaders and they are determined to provoke a civil war."

As he was writing these views, Taft was presiding at the trial of one of Deb's lieutenants, Frank M. Phelan. Phelan had come to Cincinnati to convince railway workers in Ohio and the Midwest to support their fellow workers in Chicago. When three workers on a Cincinnati railroad line were discharged for refusing to route Pullman cars, a general strike was called by all the railroad workers in the city. The court thereupon issued an injunction, which was an order forcing the workers to return to work. But when Phelan continued to incite the workers, Taft sentenced him to six months in jail for contempt of court.

During his time on the Court of Appeals, Taft made three decisions in which he outlawed the use of the boycott. Taft's interpretation of the law led labor leaders and liberals to accuse him of being antilabor. Indeed, when Taft completed the Phelan case, he felt that any political ambitions he might have had were permanently destroyed by his growing antilabor reputation.

The Advocate for Labor

In later years, when Taft was running for the presidency, supporters could cite several instances where Taft's stand had been prolabor. Two of them, the Voight case and the Narramore case, dealt with the principle of "assumed risk." Under this principle, companies could refuse to pay damages when an employee was injured in the workplace. Taft argued that an employer had a responsibility to make sure that safety devices and a safe environment were provided the employee wherever possible, and in both cases, the injured men were paid damages. These opinions became precedents for later legal decisions that resulted in the introduction of workmen's compensation and safety laws.

The Voice of Labor

Sometimes a person becomes so identified with a movement that his life story becomes the story of the movement itself. Such was the case of Samuel Gompers and the labor movement in the United States. As President of the American Federation of Labor (AFL) for 37 years, Gompers played a leading role in promoting the union cause. As a voice of reason in the labor movement, he met and worked with many Presidents, including Theodore Roosevelt, Woodrow Wilson, and William Howard Taft.

As a newly arrived immigrant boy of 13, straight from the streets of London, England, Gompers began working in the trade that his father knew, making cigars. At first they worked in cramped spaces in their home, as did many people in those days, in a system called "cottage industry." Later, they began to work in small factories. Some lacked windows, were poorly lit, and had little ventilation. The labor movement was in its infancy, but Samuel, an outgoing young man, joined the Local Cigar Makers Union No. 15.

Self-educated at night schools and well read, Sam was often picked to read to the workers, an acceptable practice in that industry. Cigar-making required skilled hands, but the mind was free to think. Often Sam read articles from the *Workingmen's Advocate* or the *National Labor Tribune.* The more he read, the more he was convinced that the conditions of the workingman had to be improved.

In 1873, a crushing depression hit the nation. Sam was a young married man with children to support. Wages were cut again and again, and when some workers dared to strike, the strikes failed.

Technology was also affecting the workers. In the cigar industry, a mold was being used to make cheap cigars, and unskilled workers began to replace the skilled cigarmaker, who hand-rolled and wrapped each cigar. Many workers tried to stop the manufacturer from using the mold, but Sam recognized that the new technology was the reality of the future. Rather than opposing the new unskilled workers, Sam Gompers urged that they be enrolled in the union.

In 1877, spurred by the success of the Cigar Makers Union to win some agreements with cigar manufacturers, the tenement workers went on strike. Sam's union had no recourse but to support their fellow unionists. For four bitter winter months, the strike went on, and when it was finally broken, Sam found himself blacklisted, unable to find work because employers would not hire him. His children were in rags and every stick of furniture had been pawned. Now Sam realized that workers had to be unified in more than just small locals.

Labor had only two legal rights—to form unions and to vote. Unlike some workers who wished to overthrow the government or wished to make the country into a socialist state, where the government owned all factories and plants, Sam believed it would be more effective to work within the system. Just after the Civil War, there had been an attempt to organize a "union of unions" called the National Labor Union, but it had not been very effective.

The Knights of Labor was another organization that attempted to organize more than a single trade. This organization, however, saw no need to use one of labor's few weapons, the strike. It did believe in the eight-hour work day, and because of that, it began to attract many workers. In 1886, when the Knights of Labor attempted to enroll cigar-makers in their union, Gompers felt the time was ripe to launch a new alliance of trade unions. That December, Gompers called a meeting in Columbus, Ohio. It was attended by delegates representing 25 organizations with a total membership of more than 300,000 men. At that meeting, the American Federation of Labor was born, and Gompers was unanimously elected as president. He would serve in that position for 37 more years.

By 1900 the AFL had more than a million members, and by 1913, more than two million. After 1905, Gompers had become so prominent as the spokesman for labor that there were few legislative committees or political conventions which did not solicit Gompers' ideas on what labor wanted. He also found no difficulty in getting an appointment to see any President of the United States. Eventually, many union demands were enacted into laws, such as the abolition of child labor and the setting of minimum standards of health and safety in factories and mines.

In the election of 1908, the AFL presented a ''Bill of Grievances'' to both political parties. The Republicans ignored the proposals, but the Democrats sought out Gompers' approval for a labor program. Though Gompers had hoped to have the union maintain its neutrality in party politics, that gesture by the Democrats pushed him to support the party. Taft and the Republicans won that election. But Wilson's Democratic victory four years later made labor a force to be reckoned with in party politics.

Despite the fact that Gompers gave Taft the nickname ''Father of Injunctions'' for his connection with the Phelan case, Gompers personally liked Taft. President Taft felt no ill will toward Gompers despite his role in the 1908 election. Taft called Gompers ''Sam'' and occasionally greeted him with, ''Hello, how are you, my old antagonist?''

Sam Gompers' efforts to keep labor producing during World War I earned him praise from the business community. Gompers had hoped that this cooperation would bear rich fruits when the war was over, but the nation was becoming more conservative, and the fact that some of the unions were falling victim to racketeers did not help labor's cause. Labor had more battles to wage, but by 1924, it was obvious that Sam Gompers would not be able to lead them. At his final

AFL convention in 1924, he declared, ''I want to . . . leave a better labor movement in America and in the world than when I entered it as a boy.''

When he died in December of that year, Gompers' body was taken to the AFL headquarters in Washington before his burial. At the hour of his funeral, the United States Senate stopped its activities while eulogies to Gompers were read.

Chapter 4

A Power in the Philippines

"The President wants me to go to the Philippine Islands," said Will as calmly as he could. "Want to go?"

Nellie's stunned silence lasted only a moment, and then she responded just as Will expected. "Yes, of course!" Nellie was not one to miss out on a great adventure and a trip to a new country.

The invitation to go to the Philippines was the last thing Taft had expected when he received a telegram from President William McKinley three days earlier asking him to come to Washington. At first, Will had hoped it might have something to do with a Supreme Court appointment, but there was no vacancy that he knew of. The offer to be president of a new commission to organize the government of the Philippine Islands was the farthest thing from Will's mind. As he described it, "He might as well have told me that he wanted me to take a flying machine."

Taft was doubtful that it was wise to abandon his judicial career, but Secretary of War Elihu Root convinced him that his country needed his services and that he needed to test his ability in a new and demanding position. The President also reassured Taft, "If you give up this judicial office at my request you shall not suffer. If I last and the opportunity comes, I shall appoint you [to the Supreme Court]."

Why was William Taft chosen for this assignment? There are two logical reasons: Taft had a reputation for unusual integrity and honesty and he was also in favor with the Republican administration. He was assured by the President that the job would last only six or nine months. But it would be almost four years before Nellie and Will would return to the United States. This time, Washington would be waiting for Will with welcoming arms and the offer of a position in the Cabinet of the new President, Theodore Roosevelt.

THE SPANISH-AMERICAN WAR

The Philippine Islands, a chain of over 7,000 islands covering an area almost as large as the state of Montana, are located in the Pacific Ocean. The largest and most important island is Luzon, where Manila, the capital of the country, is located. The Philippines had been acquired by the United States as a result of the Spanish-American War in 1898. The war had its roots in Cuba's struggle for independence. Vivid descriptions of Spanish atrocities against the local Cuban people, published in the U.S. press, aroused American sympathy for the Cubans. The American battleship *Maine* was sent to Cuba to protect U.S. citizens and property when anti-Spanish rioting broke out. When the *Maine* was attacked and sunk in Havana harbor, American patriotic fever was at the boiling point.

"Remember the *Maine*" became the rallying cry for American intervention in Cuba. President McKinley, with the support of Congress, demanded that Spain withdraw from the island and grant Cuba its independence. In retaliation, Spain declared war on the United States on April 24th. On

May 1, Commodore George Dewey and the American fleet in the Pacific steamed into Manila Bay in the Philippines and, in a leisurely morning battle, destroyed the Spanish fleet that was anchored there. Two months later, the First Volunteer Cavalry, called "the Rough Riders" and led by Teddy Roosevelt, helped to capture the city of Santiago, Cuba, while the U.S. Navy destroyed the Spanish fleet in that harbor. By July 17, the war was over.

Despite its short length, the Spanish-American War marked a turning point in American history. The United States emerged as a world power with far-flung overseas possessions and became an important player in the game of international politics. As a result of the peace treaty between the United States and Spain, the United States became a trustee of Cuba to assist that country until it could set up an independent government. Spain also gave up Guam and Puerto Rico to the United States and gave control of the Philippines to the United States for 20 million dollars.

OFF TO THE PHILIPPINES

On April 17, 1900, five members of the Philippine Commission and their families departed from San Francisco on the *Hancock* for the seven-week journey to Luzon. In addition to Will, the Taft party included Nellie, Robert, Helen, little Charles, age three, and Nellie's sister, Marie. The men of the commission had been carefully selected by McKinley, and the couples turned out to be a most compatible group.

Taft found the men well suited to the task. Two of the commissioners, General Luke E. Wright of Tennessee and Judge Henry C. Ide of Vermont, were lawyers. Professor Dean Worcester of the University of Michigan was a zoologist and had been in the islands previously. Bernard Moses, a professor at the University of California, was a historian, econo-mist, and student of politics, with special knowledge of Spanish-American countries.

While on its way to the Philippines, the *Hancock* made stops in Honolulu, Hawaii, and in Yokohama, Japan, and the group of Americans took these opportunities to do some sight-seeing. One trip to the city of Nikko to see the ancient tem-ples of Japan turned out to be a hilarious, if not embarrass-ing, experience.

The path up to the temples was long and steep, and the only means of transportation were rickshas, covered chairs on two wheels that are pulled or pushed by one man. The man assigned to Will Taft took one look at his passenger and his eyes began to roll. He gestured frantically for help, and a second man offered to push. By the time the ricksha ar-rived at the first hill, there were two or three more assistants, and by the time it arrived at the top, half of the village was engaged either in pushing, staring, or laughing at the enor-mous American visitor.

A Frigid Reception

If the members of the commission were in agreement about what they hoped to achieve in the Philippines, they faced a relentless foe with totally different ideas in the person of General Arthur MacArthur. He had been in the region since 1898 and been appointed military governor just a month be-fore the commission's arrival. The general and his staff be-lieved that a bayonet and a strong arm were the only way to deal with the native Filipinos. The general left no doubt as to his attitude toward the commission. He did not even ap-pear at the dock when the *Hancock* sailed into the harbor.

In describing their first meeting in the hot, sultry cli-mate, Taft noted that "the frigidity of the general had made his perspiration stop." Taft tried to be tactful, pointing out that the general was still in command of the military and had great power. To this MacArthur icily replied, "That would be all right, if I had not been exercising so much more power before you came." The battle lines between the military and the civilian commission were drawn.

Philippine Independence or American Colonial Government?

The commission faced not only the job of organizing a new government in the Philippines, it also had to wrestle with people who had tasted the first fruits of independence and who were angry at seeing it crushed. The movement for independence had begun in the 1880s, when sons of wealthy Filipinos who had studied abroad returned with new ideas for self-government. When the Spanish squashed the first attempts at liberal reform and executed the leaders, the Filipinos were shocked. The movement for independence now spread to the less-privileged classes, and armed revolt became a reality.

After months of fighting in 1897, the leader of the revolt, Emilio Aguinaldo, was expelled to Hong Kong. After the U.S. naval victory at Manila Bay, Admiral Dewey helped Aguinaldo and his followers to return home. Aguinaldo was confident that he had American support, and on June 12, 1898, he declared independence for the Philippines. But when American troops landed in Manila in August, they refused to let Filipino forces enter the city. Aguinaldo felt betrayed.

By the time of Taft's arrival, the countryside seethed with armed rebels. MacArthur, as the U.S. military commander, was determined to break the back of the nationalist resistance movement.

Taft saw his role quite differently. He had carefully read the report of the Schurman Commission, a group of five men sent to the Philippines in March 1899 by President McKinley to investigate the situation there. Jacob Gould Schurman, leader of the investigating team, had done a superb job of explaining the situation in the Philippines. Among the suggestions made by the Schurman Commission was a call for a marked degree of self-government for the local people under American supervision. Taft's ideas were similar.

After meeting with and listening to local leaders, Taft defined his own policy: "We hold the Philippines for the benefit of the Filipinos, and we are not entitled to pass a single act or to approve a single measure that has not that as its chief purpose."

GETTING DOWN TO BUSINESS

Taft and his colleagues now settled down to the enormous task ahead. They had three priorities for the Filipinos: to give them an education, a sense of pride and self-worth, and an opportunity to participate in government. Taft had begun to plan for an educational system even before he had left the United States. He offered the post of superintendent of education to Frederick W. Atkinson of Springfield, Massachusetts. Before his departure for the Philippines, Atkinson had combed American colleges for enthusiastic young men and women willing to venture into a new land to become "pioneers of the blackboard." Scores of young people took up the challenge.

Under Spanish rule, the only education permitted to the local people was taught by the village Catholic priests or friars. Few people could read or write, for the Spanish did not encourage such learning. No American enterprise undertaken in the Philippines received as much support and cooperation from the people as did the introduction of public schools.

Speaking English became a sign of superiority, though often the Filipinos repeated the sentences that they heard without having the slightest idea of what they were talking about. One day, in a visit to the Igorots, a Malay people living in the mountains of Luzon, Taft was greeted by the children. Civilization had barely touched these people, and he was stunned to hear their greeting: "Good Morning, Mrs. Kelly." Taft was amused but puzzled until he heard the story about Mrs. Kelly. She and her husband had lived in the area years earlier. While her husband was working to develop a gold mine, Alice Kelly started a school for the Igorot children. Each morning, they would begin the school day by saying, "Good morning, Mrs. Kelly." When Taft heard the explanation, he roared with laughter and the children laughed too, confident that they had said exactly the right thing.

Under Taft's management, education was free and English was taught as the official language of business and government. The Taft Commission allotted as much money as it could for the establishment of the public school system, and by the time the commission left, there were district schools, village and town schools, and high schools; a literate population was developing.

Nellie Helps

Nellie Taft had remained in Japan, waiting for Will to complete arrangements for the family's new home in the Philippines, when she received a special letter from her husband. "One of the things we have to do here is to extend hospitality to Filipino families of wealth and position. The army circles definitely and distinctly decline to have anything to do with them.... I need your assistance in taking a different course.... Its political effect will be considerable." If ever a woman was capable and eager to undertake this task, Nellie was that person.

Taft's success as a colonial governor was probably due to his sensitivity to the fact that the Filipinos were a proud people, resentful of anyone who made them feel as if they were an inferior race. The actions of the United States Army prior to Taft's arrival had instilled fear and distrust among the local people. Rumors abounded that the treatment of the natives would be far worse than the Spanish when the Americans controlled the land. Even the wives of Army officers had contributed to the bad feelings as they regarded the Filipinos as "unfitted to be associated with." When Nellie finally arrived, Will set out to undo this mischief and to win the Filipinos to the American side.

Though he did not approve of cockfighting, Taft urged MacArthur not to ban the activity because it was a national amusement important to the people. Cockfighting involved placing two roosters equipped with sharp spurs into a pit to fight to the death; people placed bets on the outcome of the fight. Taft also encouraged the music of the islands and suggested that money be raised to build a school of music. Taft even learned to dance the "rigodon," the national dance of the Philippines. Though the steps to this graceful dance were quite intricate and their first attempts must have made the local people laugh, Nellie — and Will, in time — mastered it.

Nellie did her part at the many official and unofficial receptions held in their home. She refused to segregate her guests by the color of their skin, and Americans and Filipinos mingled comfortably. The Filipinos were also pleased to see the members of the commission arrive at their fiestas with their wives and daughters. The anger and hostility began to change to friendship and trust as the Filipinos saw more and more of the huge lumbering man with the broad smile and hearty, belly-shaking laugh.

As the first American civil governor in the Philippines, Taft toured many areas of the islands and earned the respect and affection of the local people. (Library of Congress.)

Setting Up a Government

Though later in life Taft would gain a reputation for enjoying an unexpected nap at meetings, concerts, and receptions, he did not allow himself the luxury of a midday siesta, which was the custom in Manila. Taft felt the work was too important and too enormous to give up this time. According to the plan devised by President McKinley, Secretary of War Root, and Taft, the commission was to set up a civil government for the people of the Philippine Islands that conformed "to their customs, their habits, and even to their prejudices, to the fullest extent consistent with the accomplishment of the indispensable requisites of just and effective government."

Though there was no promise of independence, the Filipinos were guaranteed everything in the Bill of Rights except for trial by jury and the right to bear arms. They were to hold all offices for which they were qualified, and a civil service system was developed. And although Taft's commission was given the responsibility for setting up the legal system, Filipinos were invited to act as advisors on proposed legislation. Taft also hoped that, as conditions improved, the people could set up a popular assembly.

By early 1901 the commission had set up municipal governments, and the members began traveling by local railroad to many of the provinces on Luzon to see how these governments were operating. In March, the commissioners, their wives, and children, along with a group of prominent Filipinos and newspapermen, began a much longer journey around the southern islands of the country. They traveled for two months, during the hottest season of the year. The real problem was not the effect on one's skin, but on one's stomach.

Filipino hospitality nearly undid the commission. At banquets to honor the American visitors, the Filipinos served an extravagant number of courses, heavily seasoned with garlic and Spanish oil. The American guests soon learned that to refuse even one course would hurt the feelings of their host. In a letter to Elihu Root, Taft jokingly complained, "The trip is anything but a junket. It is the hardest work I have had to do since I have been out here."

By the end of the trip, Taft was convinced that the time was ripe for a civil government to take over from the military. Secretary of War Elihu Root asked Taft to develop a plan for such a government and, showing complete confidence in him, Root stated that Taft would probably be appointed as the first civil governor of the islands. The journey into the provinces had given Taft a better grasp of the variety of people, languages, and economies in the country. It also had given the people an opportunity to see the kind of man who would soon be the American civil governor of the Philippines.

The Dream of Independence Fades

The hope of Philippine independence had not died with the arrival of the Taft commission. In the islands, guerrilla warfare continued, with attacks on American military patrols. By early 1901, Emilio Aguinaldo, the rebel leader, who was hiding in the mountains of northeastern Luzon, must have realized that he and his handful of poorly equipped men could not survive much longer. Yet despite the promise of amnesty if he surrendered, Aguinaldo was determined to fight on.

However, the revolt ended on March 23, when General Frederick Funston captured Aguinaldo in a daring raid on the rebels' secret headquarters. The rebel leader was treated as an honorable prisoner of war, and General MacArthur even entertained him at his official quarters, Malacanan Palace. Shortly after, Aguinaldo took the oath of allegiance and appealed to his countrymen to accept American rule.

Chapter 5

Taft Takes Command

The Stars and Stripes gleamed in the hot sun. The sound of drums pierced the air, as did the occasional sounds of the "Star Spangled Banner" being practiced by local musicians. All was in readiness for the inauguration of William Taft as the first American civil governor of the Philippines. Thousands of people crowded into Cathedral Plaza in the heart of Manila. As Taft, General MacArthur, and Major General A. R. Chaffee, who was replacing MacArthur, strode across the square, MacArthur was in the center. On their return from the inauguration, Taft was in the center, symbolizing to the waiting crowds that Taft, representing civilian authority, was now in command of the islands. Fittingly, the date was July 4, 1901.

It was now official, and by the next day, Taft and his family had moved to Malacanan, the palace used by the Spanish governors and by General MacArthur. The move finally gave Taft the status he needed, which was important to even the educated Filipino. Malacanan was more like a summer hotel than a palace, but it delighted Nellie. She loved the Span-

ish paintings on the walls, the exquisite china for the table —
and the large staff of servants.

BAD NEWS POURS IN

Taft had barely settled in as governor when he was faced with
one calamity after another. After an exhausting tour through
the islands to establish civil governments, Will returned with
the first of a series of illnesses. The long 12-hour workdays
over the first 15 months in Manila began to take their toll
on his health. And then in September, tragedy struck.

When Taft arrived late for luncheon on September 6,
his face ashen, his body sagging, Nellie knew something terrible had happened. With a voice quivering with emotion,
Taft shared the news: "The President has been shot."

McKinley, who had been re-elected in 1900, had been
fatally wounded by an anarchist interested in overthrowing
the United States government. On September 14, 1901,
McKinley died. Theodore Roosevelt, who had been Vice-
President, was now President.

Taft knew Roosevelt on a first-name basis, and he had
confidence in him. However, in the following months, some
of Roosevelt's impetuous, autocratic manner, revealed in some
of his cables, began to upset Taft.

To add to Taft's problems, civilian authority was
challenged when 50 men of an American infantry unit were
killed in an ambush. It took Taft's quiet assurance to see that
no further major outbreaks occurred. But all of these events
took their toll; shortly after, Taft had two serious operations.
As 1901 drew to a close, Taft and his family boarded a ship
for home. He had two reasons for returning to the states. He
needed to regain his strength, and in January, 1902, he was

expected to appear before a Senate committee investigating Philippine affairs.

Dealing with the Friars

There was one problem which Taft knew would be raised at the Senate hearings. He had known about it even before he had gone to the Philippines, and he had taken it as his special responsibility, leaving other issues more suited to the expertise of his fellow commissioners. It was a delicate subject, for it concerned the Catholic Church.

When the Spanish arrived in the Philippines in the 16th century, Catholic friars (priests belonging to such religious orders as the Jesuits and Franciscans) marched with the soldiers. As the soldiers conquered the land, the friars converted the local people to Catholicism. In time, the friars and priests wielded so much power in the Philippines that they could have civilian officials removed if they did not meet with their approval. The friars controlled education, supervised the police, and owned more than 400,000 acres of the best farmland, which they rented to farmers at very high rates. The Filipino rebellion in the late 1800s was in part due to the people's hatred of the friars. When Aguinaldo became leader of the rebels, many priests were killed or imprisoned in the monasteries, and much of the friars' lands were confiscated. No rents had been paid since then.

Under the treaty with Spain, the United States had guaranteed all property rights. How could Taft restore the land to the Catholic Church without embittering the Filipinos? Since the friars held legal title to the land, it had to be purchased from the Catholic Church. In return, the Church needed to send in other clergymen, preferably enlightened American priests, in place of the Spanish friars. The big problem was how to handle the situation so that not only would the Filipinos be satisfied, but Catholic voters in the United States would be satisfied as well.

During the Senate hearings, the issue of the friars received much attention, but Taft handled the questions on this and other matters with tact and patience. Afterwards, he met with President Roosevelt, Elihu Root, and Archbishop Ireland, a leader of the Catholic Church in America. It was decided that Taft would go personally to the Vatican in Rome and try to settle the problem with Pope Leo XIII. Nellie's plan to join him was derailed when Robert Taft came down with scarlet fever. "Well," said Taft's 74-year-old mother when she heard the news, "I don't think you ought to make such a trip alone when you are so far from strong, so I think I'll go with you in Nellie's place." And she did.

From the end of May through July 1902, Taft worked hard to complete negotiations. He was received warmly by the Pope and met with high-ranking members of the Catholic Church. Though Taft had been told five million dollars was a fair price for the land, the church sought more than ten million. When Taft's compromise of $7½ million dollars was rejected, he decided to leave. Negotiations were later completed at a selling price of $7,543,000. The United States later sold the land in small parcels to native farmers. The Spanish priests were not recalled by the Church, as Taft had hoped, but as the friars and priests who had remained behind died, they were replaced by American and Filipino clergymen. Taft's tactful negotiations paid off at last.

THE LAST YEARS IN THE PHILIPPINES

Guns boomed out a welcome and the crowds gathered at the pier, straining to get their first glimpse of the governor.

"There! There! On the bridge!" The crowds cheered as

the broad figure dressed in a white suit appeared on the bridge of the ship.

Taft had been gone only six months but much had happened — and worse was yet to come. Both 1902 and 1903 witnessed a plague of cholera (an intestinal disease) in which more than 100,000 Filipinos died. The rice crop dropped by 80 percent and famine threatened the land. Starving people formed outlaw bands and a disease called rinderpest killed more than 75 percent of the farm and work animals. But what discouraged Taft most of all was the discovery of dishonesty and theft among American officials. As an example of equal American treatment for all, Taft saw to it that these men were prosecuted, and all but two were sent to prison.

"How Is the Horse?"

To add to his troubles, Taft suffered an attack of amoebic dysentery (another intestinal disease), which almost killed him. But he was determined to prove that he had the stamina for the job. A month after his illness, he decided to ride horseback under a broiling sun through the mountains of Luzon. He could not resist telegraphing Elihu Root of his achievement: "Stood up well. Rode horseback twenty-five miles to five thousand feet elevation."

The image of the 300-pound governor astride the poor sweating animal caused Root to cable back, "Referring to your telegram — how is the horse?"

The exchange of telegrams became famous because Taft loved a good joke, even when played on himself. He published the dispatch, and the local newspapers picked it up and played it to the hilt. The story would be repeated again and again during Taft's presidential campaign in 1908.

An Offer from the President

Though he was out of the United States, Taft's reputation as an administrator and a leader continued to grow. President Roosevelt was also well aware of Taft's talents as a jurist and had reasons for wanting Taft to serve on the Supreme Court. Roosevelt treated lightly the idea of equality among the three branches of government, (executive, legislative, and judicial). In 1906 he was to declare, "The President and the Congress are all very well in their way. They can see what they think they think, but it rests with the Supreme Court to decide what they have really thought." Roosevelt hoped that through his appointments to the Supreme Court, he would gain a Court that reflected his own views.

In October 1902, when a vacancy occurred, Roosevelt cabled Taft and offered him an appointment on the Court. Taft declined the offer. But in January 1903, a letter arrived from the President. "I shall have to bring you home," he wrote, "and put you on the Supreme Court. I am very sorry. I have the greatest confidence in your judgment; but after all, old fellow, if you will permit me to say so, I am President and see the whole field."

Roosevelt was a strong-willed man. Now he was to discover that Taft could be equally determined. Taft immediately cabled back that he felt he had to remain at his post because the people had confidence in him and that there were too many economic, civil, and church problems which demanded his attention. Taft also leaked out the news of Roosevelt's letter to his colleagues and some of his Filipino supporters.

In the meantime, Taft was experiencing his happiest moment in the Philippines—one perhaps even happier than his inauguration day as President of the United States in 1909.

On the morning of January 10, 1903, Nellie and Will watched with awe as the Malacanan Palace gates, once closed to stem advancing mobs, now swung open to welcome a column of Filipinos. Proudly, they strode into the courtyard, carrying banners which read *Queremos Taft!* ("We Want Taft!"). Eventually, more than 6,000 Filipinos jammed the palace courtyard. Prominent Filipino leaders, from radical labor leaders to former revolutionaries, praised Taft. One announced that the governor "had turned a dying people to the light and life of modern liberties."

As important as the demonstration was, it did not carry as much weight as the cables sent by Taft's fellow commissioners, Ide, Worcester, and Smith, and from well-known Filipinos stating that Taft's departure might have grave consequences. The bombardment of news reports and cables had its effect on Roosevelt. A terse cable to Taft followed: "All right, you shall stay where you are."

AN OFFER THAT CANNOT BE REFUSED

Taft planned to spend the next two years as civil governor in the Philippines. He hoped that, on his return to the United States, he might still be offered a Supreme Court appointment. But Roosevelt's re-election campaign kept intruding on Taft's life. Businessmen hostile to Roosevelt's ideas on trade were talking about Taft as a possible presidential candidate in 1904. Taft was furious that his name was being put forward, and he wrote to his brother Henry that he had no desire for the nomination.

Meanwhile, Roosevelt was tenacious about getting his way. And this time he would not take "No" for an answer. Secretary of War Elihu Root had informed the President that he would be resigning as of the end of 1903. Roosevelt now applied pressure, urging Taft to accept the Cabinet position. The argument that finally persuaded Taft to accept was Roosevelt's contention that he would still be in charge of the Philippines because the War Department administered the islands. But Secretary Root was concerned about Taft's health, as was his family in Manila and in the States. The illnesses he had incurred and the excessive hours of work had taken their toll. Moreover, Taft was unsure that he could support his family on the $8,000 Cabinet salary. But when his brother Charles offered to supplement Taft's income with an additional $6,000 per year, Taft accepted the Cabinet post.

On December 23, 1903, the Taft family embarked for the journey home. Will Taft may have looked longingly at the disappearing coastline, but Nellie was delighted. She had felt the offer of the Supreme Court appointment would have been a graveyard for Taft's career. But a Cabinet post, she wrote, "was in line with the kind of career I wanted for him and expected him to have." Washington was waiting for them, and Nellie was ready.

Chapter 6

A Man of Many Missions

The San Francisco earthquake, the Russo-Japanese War, the election campaign of 1906, a Cuban crisis, and the building of the Panama Canal were a few issues during the Roosevelt administration (1901–1909) in which Taft was personally involved. He was far more than simply the secretary of war. He was Roosevelt's emissary (personal agent) to foreign countries; he was also his problem-solver and legal advisor. When Secretary of State John Hay became ill, Taft was made acting secretary of state. And when Roosevelt was away from Washington, Taft was actually a temporary President of the United States. As Roosevelt once stated when leaving the nation's capital, "Things will go well in Washington. I have left Taft sitting on the lid."

The President completely trusted Taft, and Taft was utterly charmed by Roosevelt's outgoing nature and personal compliments. Taft became not only Roosevelt's capable executive assistant, he also began to agree, without question, with nearly all of Roosevelt's policies. These included foreign affairs and the regulation of American railroads and big business.

"POLITICS ... MAKES ME SICK!"

Taft's first shock was to discover that the Cabinet meetings he attended in 1904 were devoted not to matters of state, but to politics—the winning of the presidential election that year. Though Taft did not enjoy making speeches, he soon found himself making the campaign circuit in support of Roosevelt's candidacy. When the election was finally over and Roosevelt had won, Taft summed up his feelings: "A national campaign for President is to me a nightmare."

Taft's political independence was fading. His last gesture of defiance was to speak out in support of Myron Herrick, who was running for re-election as governor of Ohio. Herrick had dared to oppose the power of the Republican Party boss of Ohio, George Cox, and Taft was keenly disappointed when Herrick lost the election. Yet, before long, Taft himself would accept Cox's support.

In 1906, Roosevelt called on his Cabinet members to campaign again because he needed the security of a Republican Congress to carry out his ideas. Once again, Taft took to the road, making speeches from Illinois to Wyoming and from Kansas to Texas. Roosevelt got his congressional victory, but Taft commented bitterly, "Politics, when I am in it, makes me sick!"

FOREIGN DEALINGS

The California gold rush of 1849 created great interest in the narrow isthmus of land in Central America called Panama, officially a part of nearby Colombia. Many prospectors going to California had chosen to cross Panama instead of using the difficult overland trail across the United States. Seeing the possibilities of economic gain from a water route through

Panama, the French in 1879 began digging a canal. The venture failed, partly because of disease and mismanagement, but also because of constant riots and changes in the local administration in Panama.

Then the United States began negotiating with Colombia to build a canal. When Colombia delayed in approving a canal treaty, the United States seized the chance to support a Panamanian movement for independence. In November 1903 the United States formally recognized the independence of Panama. In return, a treaty was signed with the new nation, giving the United States control of an area called the Canal Zone and the right to preserve the independence of the new republic.

A new organization, called the Isthmus Canal Commission, was formed and Roosevelt placed Taft in charge of overseeing the building of the new canal. Taft's first chore was to take a trip to the Canal Zone to assure the Panamanians of America's good intentions. He informed them that local people would profit from the sale of goods and services to workmen on the project. He confirmed that goods would enter Panamanian ports, where duties on goods would be collected for the treasury of the new government. Taft's manner and the hopes of economic profit seemed to satisfy the local people.

Perhaps Taft's greatest contribution to the Panama Canal was his support of Dr. William Gorgas and Major George W. Goethals. From his work as sanitation officer in Cuba, Gorgas had decided that a certain mosquito was the major carrier of yellow fever, though many scoffed at the idea. In his same role in the Canal Zone, Gorgas drained ditches and other breeding places for mosquitoes and, within two years, yellow fever was erased and even malaria was brought under control. Without the tremendous loss of men and time, work on the project now moved speedily ahead.

When the private business efforts of the Isthmus Canal Commission proved ineffective, Taft suggested to the President that the project be given to the Army Corps of Engineers. Goethals was Taft's choice for chief engineer. The secretary of war had met Goethals on his tour of the Canal Zone and had been impressed by his grasp of the situation. It was no easy task to keep up the morale of 30,000 men working far from home under very difficult conditions, but Goethals proved to be a superb administrator as well as an excellent engineer. When the canal was opened in 1914, Goethals was appointed the first civil governor of the Canal Zone.

Return to the Philippines

Taft had promised he would return to the Philippines, and in July 1905, he did, bringing with him a shipload of 30 influential congressmen as well as 50 others, including newspaper correspondents and President Roosevelt's irrepressible daughter, Alice. Taft was a hearty, enthusiastic leader of the expedition, but he had a hard time keeping up with Alice Roosevelt, who livened up the journey with her wit, her pranks, and her glamorous masquerade costumes.

The trip was intended to use Taft's popularity with the Filipinos to halt a rising tide of cries for independence. Taft himself was not convinced that the Filipinos were ready for such a move. But he was eager to have the congressmen see the islands, meet the people, and, hopefully, support his ideas for legislation that would benefit the Philippines.

The trip proved to be a great success on all counts. Taft summed it up this way: "We took eighty people with us and came back so harmonious that everyone was able to speak to everyone else."

The bountiful Filipino hospitality delighted Taft's boatload of friends, but it was a disaster for Taft. By the time he arrived back in the United States, he weighed 325 pounds. "I am convinced," he said, "that this undue drowsiness is due to the accumulation of flesh.... Were I appointed to the bench I fear I could not keep awake in my present condition." He realized something had to be done and willingly put himself into the hands of a doctor. Taft now began a careful diet and rode horseback daily. Within six months he was down to a more acceptable weight—250 pounds—and felt infinitely better. The only setback was one to his purse, for he found the alterations of his clothing a costly affair.

A Secret Pact

What his companions on the ship steaming to Manila had *not* known was that Taft was on a secret mission for the President. Roosevelt was convinced that peace in the Orient was important to the United States, not only for the security of the Philippines, but to European peace as well. In 1904 war had broken out between Russia and Japan. Both countries had suffered severe losses of life, and the military expenditures had drained their economies. Behind the scenes, Roosevelt had been asked to negotiate a peace between the two nations.

The President asked his secretary of war to stop in Tokyo enroute to the Philippines to meet secretly with the Japanese premier, Count Tara Katsura. Taft's mission was to reach some agreements with the Japanese prior to a peace conference scheduled to be held in New Hampshire in August.

During Taft's meeting with the Japanese premier, a secret pact was agreed upon. The United States would not object to Japanese domination of Korea, and Japan would not interfere in the Philippines. The Japanese also expected that as part of the final agreement with Russia, Japan would receive reparations (payments for war damages) from Russia. However, by the time Taft and his shipload of friends returned to the United States, the Japanese learned that they would not receive reparations, and they were outraged. Anti-American riots and demonstrations broke out in Tokyo. These, in turn, created anti-Japanese feelings among Americans, particularly in California, where the majority of Japanese immigrants had settled. At times, newspapers added fuel to the fire by writing about the "yellow peril," the possibility of hordes of foreigners from the Orient taking over the West Coast.

In 1907 Taft made a second journey to the Philippines, supposedly to attend the opening of the Filipino assembly, which would give the people a measure of self-government. But the President also wanted Taft to stop in Japan in order to smooth relations with that nation. Anti-Japanese demonstrations were again erupting in California. School authorities in San Francisco had even ruled that Japanese children could not attend classes with white children. Roosevelt was as angry with California as he was with Japan.

In his behind-the-scenes meetings, Taft listened to Japan's complaints. The Japanese objected violently to any treaty which admitted Europeans and restricted Japanese emigration to America. Taft won a verbal agreement in which the Japanese agreed to limit the number of passports it would issue, particularly to Honolulu, where more than 65,000 Japanese people worked. In return, Taft promised to help stop anti-Japanese agitation in the United States and to get Congress to accept the "gentlemen's agreement" between the two nations. Though the situation improved for the moment, the problem would plague both Taft and Woodrow Wilson after him, during their respective presidential terms.

THE PACE QUICKENS

Taft was feeling more and more at home in the environment of the White House. His hearty chuckle echoed through the halls. A bond of friendship developed among Roosevelt, Taft, and Secretary of State Elihu Root, to the point where not only did they call themselves "The Three Musketeers," but so did the press and cartoonists. Taft seemed to thrive on the excitement and the pace of the work. He managed to rise to each emergency promptly and effectively.

One such instance occurred when, shortly after midnight on April 16, 1906, Taft was awakened by a telephone call from the White House. San Francisco had suffered a catastrophic earthquake! The city was in flames. For once, Taft ignored the law. The emergency could not wait. Without the consent of Congress (which later gave its approval), he ordered Army equipment, such as tents and medical supplies, to be shipped to the stricken city. Taft's prompt action helped to alleviate much of the original shock and suffering.

CRISIS IN CUBA

The Spanish-American War may have been fought for Cuban independence, but within three years, the United States placed severe limits on Cuban self-government. The Platt Amendment, passed by Congress in 1901, stated that Cuba could not make treaties giving control to foreign nations, that Cuba would give a naval base, Guantanamo Bay, to the United States, and that the United States could intervene in Cuba "for preservation of Cuban independence." In 1902, Tomás Palma was sworn in as the first president of the Republic of Cuba. The first Palma government included members from both the Moderate and Liberal parties. Four years later, after Palma had eliminated the Liberals from his Cabinet in order to push for a more conservative domestic program, rumblings of revolution began.

Roosevelt, busy with mid-term elections, did not want the Cuban problem to affect American politics. But when Palma realized he had lost control and could no longer protect life or property, he called for American troops.

Taft was enjoying a much-needed vacation with his family at their summer home in Murray Bay, Quebec, Canada, when he received a call from Roosevelt. Rushing to Washington, Taft met with the President. The question in Taft's mind was: Could the President intervene in Cuban affairs without the consent of Congress?

To the Rescue

Roosevelt would not consider asking Congress for its consent. In Roosevelt's mind, the President believed he had the constitutional power to deal independently in matters of foreign affairs. "It is for the enormous interest of this government to strengthen and give independence to the executive in dealing with foreign powers... Therefore the important thing to do is for a President who is willing to accept responsibility to establish precedents which successors may follow." Roosevelt's interpretation of the executive powers in the Constitution was one with which future Presidents, as well as Congress, would continue to wrestle.

Roosevelt knew the nation was tiring of its experiences with imperialism, of taking responsibility for territories and people all over the globe. He wanted Taft to settle the Cuba issue quickly and with as little military intervention as possible. Roosevelt's orders were to "do anything that is necessary... but try to do it in as gentle a way as possible." But when Taft arrived in Cuba, he realized that intervention would be necessary.

Palma had had enough. He wished only to resign. As Taft described it, "Palma and the Moderates will now take away their dolls and not play." Yet there was nobody in the Liberal Party strong enough to hold the country together. On September 29, 1906, Taft declared himself provisional governor of Cuba. He tried to soften the blow to Cuban pride by making sure that he signed all documents, "Republic of Cuba under the Provisional Administration of the United States."

Taft made a plea to opposition leaders to turn in their arms, and they agreed to cooperate. Cuban fears that the United States wanted to annex the island were calmed by the actions of the large, kindly man sent by the American President. A month later, Taft was able to turn over his position to Charles E. Magoon, and Cuban Liberals took over control of their country.

Taft's years as a Cabinet member had broadened his experience in foreign affairs, administration, government—and politics. Now he faced the biggest decision of his life—to be a Supreme Court justice or President of the United States. Both were available. Which should he choose?

Chapter 7

Nellie Gets Her Way

D inner at the White House had been a most pleasant affair. The Secretary of War and Mrs. Taft were obviously delighted when, after dinner, the President invited them to join him in the library. Roosevelt settled back in an easy chair and closed his eyes. In a deep, mysterious voice, he intoned, "I am the seventh son of a seventh daughter. . . . I have clairvoyant powers. I see a man weighing 350 pounds. There is something heavy over his head. I cannot make out what it is. . . it looks like the presidency; then again, it looks like the chief justiceship."

"Make it the presidency!" cried Mrs. Taft.

"Make it the chief justiceship," said Mr. Taft.

MAKING A DECISION

The President had offered Taft an appointment to the Supreme Court on several occasions. Each time, Taft had turned it down, saying, "I have work with the canal and the Philippines that I must finish first."

And as early as 1906, it was obvious that, with Roosevelt's backing, Taft could have the Republican presidential nomination in 1908 if he wanted it. But Will Taft squirmed, wriggled, and suggested other candidates. He found it almost impossible to make the decision. When Nellie stated in no uncertain terms that she did not want him to take the Court position, Roosevelt offered to meet with her to discuss the situation. By the time the meeting with Nellie was over, she had convinced Roosevelt that Taft should run for the presidency. To Will Taft, Roosevelt merely said, "The choice is yours, of course."

By 1907 it was obvious that Taft had to make a decision. Any presidential campaign required an organization and a group of delegates pledged to his candidacy long before the actual nominating convention. Charles Taft, with great confidence in his brother, began organizing a campaign in March of 1908. By July, the organization was well under way.

Trying to maintain the ethical standards he had always set for himself, Taft refused to make a deal with his old enemy, Joseph Foraker, who was now a senator. Foraker promised to support Taft for the presidency if Taft would support him for his senatorial re-election. When Taft refused, a fight was on. Despite bitter opposition from Foraker, the Ohio Republican State Central Committee endorsed Taft's candidacy. No public announcement had been made, but it was now very clear that Taft was formally a candidate for the highest office in the land.

To Follow the Leader or Not?

Roosevelt had made Taft his choice for the presidency because Teddy believed his secretary of war was the best man to continue the "Roosevelt policies." He supported Taft because he felt they both had the same ideas, ideals, and objectives. Taft was appreciative of Roosevelt's efforts on his behalf. However, Mrs. Taft was not so sure that Taft's close association with Roosevelt would benefit her husband as he campaigned and took over as chief executive.

The two men may have agreed in principle, but their style of governing was totally different. Teddy Roosevelt was quick, aggressive, and decisive. Will Taft was slow, deliberate, and cautious in making judgments. One biographer described Taft as being "too lazy to hunt and Roosevelt as too restless to fish."

More important was their attitudes toward the chief executive's role. Roosevelt deemed the presidency the most important of the three branches of government. Taft, ever the judge, believed in the constitutional point of view—equality among the three branches.

INTO THE FRAY

Taft's only rival for the Republican presidential nomination was Governor Charles Evans Hughes of New York. But Roosevelt was not about to let Hughes steal Taft's place. Hughes scheduled a major address on January 31, 1908. With great cunning, the President chose the same day to send a scorching message to Congress, an assault on corrupt corporations and a plea for greater morality in the business world. The next day's newspaper headlines blared Roosevelt's message; Hughes' carefully wrought speech and his presidential aspirations were buried on the back pages.

The Republican National Convention opened July 16. Taft's nomination seemed assured when the Ohio delegation marched in displaying a huge banner with a portrait of Taft's smiling face. But by the second day, Nellie, receiving the news by phone, was getting nervous. During a speech given by the convention chairman, Senator Henry Cabot Lodge of Massachusetts, he mentioned Roosevelt's name. Suddenly the hall erupted with shouts of "Four, four, four more years!" The demonstration lasted for 40 minutes.

Nellie could not conceal her disappointment when the demonstration following the nominating speech for her husband lasted only 25 minutes. But the final results pleased her. By late afternoon, Taft had won and a motion was passed to make the nomination unanimous.

Though Taft realized the selection of a Vice-President was important and he had some names to put forward, he made no fight to get his way. As a result, a political hack whose chief virtue was his nickname, "Sunny Jim" Sherman, was chosen.

Opposing Taft as the Democratic candidate was William Jennings Bryan, making his third and last run for the presidency. He was a brilliant orator and regarded as a champion of such liberal causes as voting rights for women and the popular election of senators. But in his speeches, Bryan failed to make a clear distinction between those ideas of Roosevelt he was willing to accept and those he rejected. Though Taft's speeches were often far too long and lacked the fire of Bryan's and Roosevelt's, his honest statements and his humor held his audiences.

On the Campaign Trail

Taft's chuckle was his greatest asset and was probably the most infectious in the history of politics. It began with a quivering of Taft's big belly, a momentary pause in his speech, and a slow grin spreading over his face. Then the chuckle bubbled forth and ended in a deep belly laugh in which an audience invariably joined in—whether they understood the point of the joke or not.

In his campaign speeches, Taft hammered away at one theme. He praised Roosevelt for being an active and innovative President who urged legislation in many new areas. Taft made it clear that the chief function of his administration would be to assure that the laws passed during Roosevelt's presidency would continue to operate smoothly and effectively. Later, critics would turn on Taft and use this theme to call him a "stand pat" President, lacking vision and energy.

Though Taft had resigned from the Cabinet at the end of July, he put off the ordeal of campaigning until September. By election day, he was completely exhausted from 40 days of nonstop public speaking. The election gave Taft 321 electoral votes to Bryan's 162. But Taft had less than one-half of the lead in popular votes that Roosevelt had garnered four years earlier. It was an omen of the unrest and turbulence that lay ahead for the new President.

Break with Tradition

President and Mrs. Roosevelt had graciously invited the Tafts to spend the night before the inauguration at the White House. A small dinner was held. Among the guests was Captain Archie Butt, the senior aid who would continue to serve Taft as faithfully as he had served Roosevelt. Conversation was strained, and Mrs. Roosevelt seemed a little depressed, perhaps because her husband was leaving shortly after the inauguration for an extended African safari.

The next morning heralded further problems. The wind howled outside and snow blanketed the streets of Washington. Instead of holding the traditional ceremony outdoors, the inauguration had to be changed to a jam-packed Senate chamber instead.

The three Taft children and Mrs. Taft viewed the proceedings from the gallery. Robert and Helen were grown up enough to look forward eagerly to seeing the ceremony. Eleven-year-old Charlie, who was concerned that he might find his father's inaugural speech boring, carried a copy of *Treasure Island*. His mother was pleased to note that the new

William Howard Taft has been the only American to serve as both President of the United States and Chief Justice of the Supreme Court. (Library of Congress.)

President's speech must have been better than expected, for Charlie never opened the book.

By the time Taft finished his inaugural speech, the sun was shining. It was customary for the new President and the former President to ride together in a carriage both before and after the ceremony. But Roosevelt decided that he would change the ritual. He felt that after the inauguration, the new President should have the spotlight and the former President should quietly retire in a separate carriage.

On learning of the new plans, Nellie announced that she would take the place of honor beside her husband. Never before had a First Lady accompanied her husband from the inauguration. Some members of Congress were miffed that they were not offered the place of honor. Others saw it as a sign of friction between the Roosevelts and the Tafts. A break would occur between the two men at a later time, but not on that day.

Chapter 8

Off to a Poor Start

What was the condition of the country that Taft inherited from Roosevelt in March 1909? What were the problems facing the new President? The United States was losing its rural nature, with more and more people leaving the farm and small towns for the sprawling industrial cities. Immigration was still relatively unrestricted. One out of every seven Americans was foreign-born. Most of the newcomers settled in the eastern cities, creating housing, school, and sanitation problems.

More and more skilled workers were organizing or joining labor unions, and corporations were rapidly increasing in size. Despite competition, one percent of the industrial companies were producing 44 percent of all manufactured goods, and a small group of financiers monopolized or controlled the railroads. With the establishment of the Ford Motor Company and General Motors Corporation, the automobile had become big business.

Four-fifths of all blacks lived in the South. Segregation existed in schools, churches, labor organizations, and in such public facilities as hotels, restaurants, and toilets. Though radio and movies had been developed in the early 1900s, they were only available to a few people.

The Women's Christian Temperance Union (WCTU) was pushing for an amendment to the Constitution to stop the sale of liquor. At state levels, organizations were fighting for suffrage (voting rights) for women, better labor laws, and "equal pay for equal work." By the end of Taft's term, 14 states had given women the right to vote. (Though Taft did speak before a convention of the National American Woman Suffrage Association, he was hissed when he said that most women were not interested in obtaining suffrage.)

There was also a strong progressive movement led by Robert La Follette of Wisconsin. In many states, direct primary elections were being used to take political power away from party bosses. The direct primary gave voters an opportunity to offer their own candidates for office rather than merely approving the choices of the politicians, which previously had been decided in party caucuses (private political meetings).

Laws were enacted forcing employers to pay compensation for workers injured in industrial accidents, and child labor laws were passed except in the southern states. There was also a drive to use legal measures to conserve forests and waterpower.

THE POWER OF THE PRESS

The early 1900s was also a period that saw the rise of "yellow journalism," when unsavory publishers, eager to increase the sale of their newspapers and magazines, were willing to print sensational stories about public officials and government misconduct, sometimes at the expense of the truth.

While Roosevelt had demonstrated a real flair for using the press to mold public opinion, Taft never learned to use the press to his advantage. Roosevelt was the first President to send up "trial balloons." It was simple. He would call in one or two favorite reporters and, pledging them not to divulge the source, he would give them some information about a policy he was considering. The correspondents would "leak" the story, revealing that "the President, according to close intimates," was about to take the following action. If the public reaction to the article was favorable, Roosevelt would go ahead with his plans. If the reaction was negative, he would quietly forget the matter. Roosevelt was not about to make a fight for an issue until either the public was ready or had been fully prepared.

Taft, on the other hand, seemed insensitive to public opinion and the power of the press. He failed to use newspapers and magazines to help him achieve his goals. Within a month of his inauguration, there were complaints that the President was withholding news. He disliked meeting with reporters, and they soon realized this fact. When they were unsuccessful in getting their news from Taft, they turned to other sources, including men who formed his opposition. What news the press did print often described Taft's tennis game, his golf scores, and his horseback rides, items which, in time, came to bore both the reporters and the people as well.

DISSENSION IN THE RANKS

It was Taft's misfortune to come into office at a time when the Republican Party was torn with dissension. Even before taking office, Taft knew he faced a split in the party. On one side were the conservatives, dedicated to the wealthy, big business, and the political game; they wished to maintain control of the party and keep things as they were. On the other side were the "insurgents," a group of younger men mostly from the West and Midwest. These congressmen opposed the policies of the majority of the party and refused to take orders from their leaders on legislative measures with which they did not agree. These young Republican rebels had come into office as reformers in their own states and were supported by factory workers, cattlemen, miners, and farmers.

Republican power in Congress was in the hands of two figures: Joseph (Uncle Joe) Cannon of Illinois, Speaker of the House, and Nelson Aldrich of Rhode Island, Republican boss of the Senate. Cannon was scornful of any Republican seeking change, and Taft personally found him to be unscrupulous and vulgar. As majority leader, Cannon controlled the party with an iron fist, cutting off debate and removing members from a committee if they did not do his bidding. As chairman of the powerful House Rules Committee, he could stifle any opposition by seeing that the only bills brought to the floor were those which met his approval.

Aldrich was equally intolerant with those who did not agree with him. As a self-made millionaire, he sided with big business and had the support of the steel, oil, and railroad barons. He bitterly opposed unions, believing that "Christian men... given control of the property interests of this country... [would protect] the rights and interests of the laboring man."

Taft's initial thoughts were to join the insurgents in trying to unhorse Cannon and Aldrich. Unfortunately, he took Roosevelt's advice to support Cannon and Aldrich against the insurgents in order to win their backing in his first fight. Taft chose the wrong bedfellows—and the wrong issue on which to make his reputation as President.

THE TARIFF ISSUE

Taft never had the traditional presidential "honeymoon." The first 100 days of an administration is usually a time when Congress and the nation are willing to give the new President

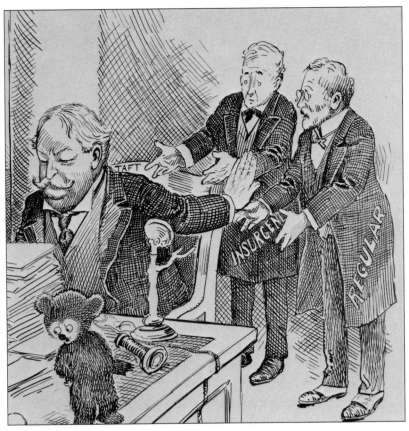

On taking office, President Taft faced a Republican Party that was split into two camps, the conservative Regulars and a younger, more liberal group called the Insurgents. The Insurgents protested against many of the actions of the party Regulars. As depicted in this cartoon, entitled "Taking No Sides," Taft tried unsuccessfully to remain neutral in the intraparty fight. (Library of Congress.)

a chance to prove his mettle. Unfortunately, Taft chose an issue which was a no-win situation then and remains the same even today—the tariff.

From the Civil War on, the Republican Party had been associated with the idea of a protective tariff. Tariffs, sometimes called duties or customs, are taxes on goods imported (brought into) a country. They serve two purposes. The first is to collect monies or revenues. The second is to protect domestic industry. By placing taxes on imports, these items cost more, allowing domestic producers to be more competitive with foreign goods, increase profits, employ more people, and increase wages. A tariff is also supposed to protect new or "infant" industries that are just getting started.

In reality, however, a protective tariff is often used to protect older industries that are no longer able to compete profitably against foreign imports. Those opposing such a tariff argue that consumers end up paying higher prices and, in the end, commerce between nations decreases as foreign nations retaliate by taxing American exports.

The Republican platform (position on national issues) of 1908 included a general statement about tariffs that left the issue open to several interpretations. But in his election campaign, Taft had clearly promised to revise the tariffs downward. He was not the first President to do so. Grover Cleveland had argued in 1893 that lowering tariff rates would lower the cost of living for workers, help international trade, and destroy this special privilege, which favored the industrial class. Later, William McKinley also tried to reduce tariff rates, but by means of mutual agreements with other nations rather than through congressional legislation. Neither President had been successful. During Roosevelt's tenure, nothing was done, for Roosevelt shunned the tariff issue as a politically explosive subject.

One Blunder After Another

Roosevelt was right—the tariff was a very explosive subject. Taft's big mistake was in trusting Cannon and Aldrich, each of whom, in private conversations with the President, promised to help him achieve lower tariffs. Shortly after his inauguration, Taft called a special session of Congress to revise tariff rates. From the very beginning, the new President made one political blunder after another. Instead of a stirring call to action at the opening session, he sent Congress a bland two-minute message. Because he failed to send a strong message, the Republican insurgents, who sided with him on this issue, believed Taft had defected to the conservatives. Moreover, the President lacked detailed information on what was really included in the costs of manufacturing each item under discussion. Without such data, it was hard to determine what the tariff on any item should be.

Most important, Taft failed to use political clout to get his way. He could have called in senators and representatives and refused to approve appointments of postmasters and other patronage jobs unless they agreed to vote his way. His politically astute Vice-President, Sherman, argued, "Shut them [the recalcitrant senators and representatives] all off. . . . The innocent can work on the guilty and it can all be done without any personal threat. . . Have it announced that the party is committed to this reform bill. . . and that any person who tries to defeat the party wishes must necessarily be considered hostile." To which Taft replied, "I hate to use patronage as a club unless I have to."

When La Follette called Taft to tell him the tariff bill did not match his campaign pledge, Taft threatened to veto it. Yet when La Follette urged Taft to send a firm message to Congress, his only comment was, "I don't much believe in a President's interfering with the legislative department while it is doing its work."

A Mangled Bill

Cannon and Aldrich, each in their own way, undermined Taft's efforts. Each ended up supporting his own political interests rather than Taft's. So did most members of Congress, who voted for the interests of their own constituencies.

Taft thoroughly enjoyed one of the privileges of the presidency—throwing out the first ball of the season for the Washington Senators baseball team. (Library of Congress.)

As the mangled bill neared completion, Taft finally met with several members of the House. He suggested a series of downward revisions in tariff rates that had been recommended to him by La Follette. Some of Taft's suggestions were accepted, and the final bill did contain more downward than upward revisions, but it hardly matched his original expectations. The bill, called the Payne-Aldrich Bill, was loaded with several additions, including the first tax on corporations and the establishment of a Tariff Commission. In the end, Taft could not veto the measure because it would have destroyed whatever relationship he still had with Republican leaders and widened the rift in the party.

Mending Fences

The newspapers and disappointed congressmen made their dissatisfaction with the Payne-Aldrich Bill known promptly. Taft realized that if he ever expected to win on other issues and be re-elected, he would first have to win the approval of the American people. Belatedly, he decided to go on an extensive personal tour across the country to explain the tariff and his future plans.

However, he first took a month's vacation in Beverly, Massachusetts. He delayed writing his speeches so long that Archie Butt, now Taft's personal aide, said, "If the President continues to transact business as he is transacting it now, he will be about three years behind when the fourth of March 1913 [the end of his term of office] rolls around."

Taft began his cross-country trip September 14, 1909, but before the month was over, he had blundered again. In a hastily written speech, he gave a fairly detailed defense of the Payne-Aldrich Bill to the people of Winona, Minnesota. He stated that the bill did not accomplish all he had hoped for and that it was certainly far from perfect. He should have stopped there, for his next 25 words proved to be the most damaging he ever uttered. "On the whole, however, I am bound to say that I think the Payne bill is the best bill that the Republican party ever passed."

The next day, big, bold newspaper headlines read, "PAYNE ACT BEST TARIFF IN HISTORY, STATES TAFT." The detailed story could be read below, but most people, reading only the headlines, were enraged. Disgruntled factory workers, farmers, and office workers facing the highest cost of living in the nation's history roundly criticized the President. Democrats, too, made the most of the headlines.

The journey continued, but Taft's capacity for getting himself into trouble continued as well. Accompanied by Archie Butt, Taft made speeches at county fairs, at the laying of cornerstones, and from the rear of his train. At one stop, the ladies of the WCTU presented him with an elegant dish of trout. Taft could not resist. With a twinkle in his eye, he asked, "Is there anything intoxicating in the fish?" The ladies did not see the joke – at all! On returning to his carriage, the President noted, "It is my experience. . . that the good women who head the temperance movement are usually devoid of humor."

The 13,000-mile trip included an exchange of visits at El Paso, Texas, and Juarez, Mexico, between Taft and President Porfirio Diaz of Mexico. Diaz had ruled his nation for more than 30 years, but his regime was tottering. American businessmen who had invested heavily in Mexico found it convenient to support the dictator, who had permitted huge profits to be made in his country. Taft hoped that the visit would strengthen Diaz's government. But two years later, progressives and liberals in Mexico overthrew Diaz and elected a new President, Francisco Madero.

A NEAR TRAGEDY

"The President," wrote Archie Butt, "looked like a great stricken animal. I have never seen greater suffering or pain on a man's face."

Those who were with Taft that day would never forget the look of anguish on the President's face when he was told that Nellie was lying in the cabin of the presidential yacht, unable to speak or move. She had experienced a stroke. It was only two months since he had taken office, but the aggravation of the tariff issue and the subsequent unfavorable publicity had made Taft decide to spend a few hours relaxing on the presidential yacht on the Potomac River. Nellie's efforts during the election campaign and the excitement of the move to the White House had taken its toll on her.

The first 24 hours after Nellie's stroke were probably the most frightening for Taft. They had been married almost 25 years, and their marriage had been a source of great strength and happiness to the huge, genial gentleman. Anyone who did not have the First Lady's grit and determination might have succumbed to the illness that affected her speech and the use of her right arm and leg.

For over a year, Taft lost his most important political advisor, and much of his energy was sapped in his worries about Nellie's health. But she fought her way back. Within a few months, she was well enough to find time to arrange for an extra-large bathtub to be installed in the White House after the President had become stuck in the regular one.

By the time the winter social season was in full swing, Nellie was well enough to appear in public. However, she was wise enough to know that she could not stand for hours greeting guests without a rest, so she devised little tricks to give herself a respite. She would ask for a glass of water and take a long time sipping it; or she would pretend to have trouble with the flowers on her gown and excuse herself to take care of them. Other times, she would just sit down and let the crowds pass by. She also learned that slippers with low heels, though not as stylish, were far more comfortable and enabled her to stay on her feet longer.

An Active Social Life

When she was home from college, Helen Taft acted as her father's hostess during Nellie's illness. Early in the winter of 1910, her mother decided to arrange two social affairs for Helen's official debut into society. One was an afternoon "At Home"; the other was a ball to which hundreds of Washington's "best" young people were invited. Taft loved the ball, and he stayed up until two in the morning displaying his talents as a dancer. Although he might doze off at a meeting the next day, the President was an enthusiastic party-goer. During his administration, Washington society had to admit that the social scene was vastly improved.

For the Tafts, the most cherished memory of their White House years was the party Nellie gave for their 25th wedding anniversary. It was an evening garden party held in June 1911, and more than 4,000 people came. In Nellie's words, "A more brilliant throng was never gathered in this country." Colored lanterns glowed from the trees, fountains displayed every color of the rainbow, and even the weather cooperated to make Nellie's dream come true. Like a queen, she stood beside the President wearing a diamond tiara, her husband's anniversary gift.

Nellie also wanted to leave her mark on Washington and to help beautify it and add to its cultural life. Her interest in music led her to convert Potomac Park into a place where Washingtonians could meet and, several evenings a week, could listen to band concerts. Remembering the pleasures of the Cherry Blossom Festival in Japan, she arranged for such an event for Potomac Park. When the mayor of Tokyo learned of her plans, he sent 2,000 young cherry trees. Nellie Taft's Cherry Blossom Festival continues today to be one of the highlights of the spring season in Washington.

One of the great social events held at the White House during the Taft administration was the 25th wedding anniversary party of the President and his wife in 1911, when this family picture was taken. (Library of Congress.)

Chapter 9

A Parting of the Ways

Did Taft say it openly or not? Did he say it and forget his promise? In any event, Taft had given Roosevelt and his Cabinet the distinct impression that he would retain Roosevelt's Cabinet members when he took office. Taft insisted, however, that he had always intended to make up his own mind and select his own Cabinet, choosing the best men available. It was true that he sought advice from Nelson Aldrich, the Republican leader in the Senate, but he had not consulted with Roosevelt or other powerful party leaders. The new Cabinet had only two carryovers from the Roosevelt days; the other positions were filled mainly by lawyers, people with whom Taft felt comfortable. But in some quarters there were snide remarks that Taft's Cabinet decisions were a rejection of the previous administration.

One of the men replaced was James R. Garfield, secretary of the interior and son of assassinated former President James A. Garfield. Of all the Cabinet members, the most controversial appointment and the one which would eventually create a major crisis, was that of Richard Ballinger, Garfield's replacement. An expert in mining and land law, Ballinger had served as a commissioner of the General Land

Office under Roosevelt. The battleground would turn out to be the growing interest in conservation.

THE CONSERVATION MOVEMENT

The conservation movement began in the West with a call for a federal waterpower development program, including irrigation, navigation, and flood control. Early in 1900, both parties called for such a program, to be financed from the sale of public western lands. Because the program affected the water supply, the grazing of cattle and the cutting of timber were prohibited in national forests. A need developed for scientific forest management. When Roosevelt came to the White House, he made conservation of the remaining public lands a matter of high priority. He was aided in his plans by a young man who worshipped Roosevelt and was a fanatic on the subject of conservation—Clifford Pinchot.

There was no question that Pinchot, chief of the United States Forest Service, knew more about forestry than anyone else in the country. Pinchot and Roosevelt went about their crusade to conserve public lands, paying little heed to Congress, achieving their ends mainly by executive order. Though Taft believed in the need for conservation of such lands, he also believed that the Interior Department and the Executive branch should use only those powers expressly authorized by the law.

In August 1909, Pinchot was informed by a public land inspector, Louis Glavis, that he had "damaging and conclusive evidence" showing "official misconduct of Secretary Ballinger." Friction between Pinchot and Ballinger had existed for some time. Moreover, Pinchot was a close friend of Garfield's and had been disappointed to see him lose his Cabinet post. Pinchot was intrigued by Glavis' report and began to follow up on the information. When Taft learned of this, he interceded, asking Pinchot not to take any hasty public action. Pinchot threatened to resign, knowing full well that such a resignation would brand Taft's administration as being against conservation.

Pinchot Versus Ballinger

The battle took place over coal lands in Alaska. A prospector, Clarence Cunningham, had secured claims on 5,000 acres before Pinchot, in 1906, had withdrawn more than seven million acres of these lands for the government. Glavis' suspicions were based on word of mouth. He had heard that Cunningham's land, along with other claims, would eventually be taken over by the Guggenheims, one of the nation's biggest mining corporations. From this, Glavis had concluded that the coal fields of Alaska would soon be exploited by eastern industrialists.

The only evidence which was definitely true was the superficial fact that Ballinger had acted as attorney for Cunningham and other speculators *after* he had resigned as land commissioner and before he joined the Cabinet.

Just before beginning his cross-country tour in 1909, the President carefully studied the evidence for three days. He then wrote a lengthy report to the Cabinet clearing Ballinger of any misconduct. But once again, Taft failed to take any public action until it was too late. While Taft was on tour, the Forest Service "leaked" some of Glavis' charges to the public, and an article appeared in *Collier's Weekly* under Glavis' name. The information soon appeared in some of the muckraking magazines and newspapers. Taft and Ballinger were scathingly accused of being anticonservation. Had Taft made his judgment known to the people, he might have stopped the slanderous charges, but he did not.

Bypassing the President

When the truth began to emerge, Pinchot wrote a letter to a senator seeking leniency for two of his subordinates whom, he had to admit, had acted improperly. The letter was read openly in the Senate. Pinchot's appeal to the legislative branch rather than to the President completely defied the proper channels of authority. Taft was left with no other recourse. He fired both Pinchot and Glavis.

Ballinger demanded a congressional investigation to clear his name, and after four months, a joint committee of Congress declared Ballinger innocent of any wrongdoing. But the damage was done. Much of the public saw the hearings as a "whitewash" of Ballinger and the Taft administration.

Pinchot raced to Europe to meet Roosevelt as he was returning from his African trip. Pinchot announced to Roosevelt that Taft had turned away from all of the former President's conservation policies. This time Taft could read the signs. He knew he lacked the support of the general public, which Roosevelt had enjoyed. If Pinchot and other Roosevelt allies were successful, Taft might soon lose the backing of Roosevelt himself.

On June 30, 1910, Roosevelt visited Taft at the summer White House in Beverly, Massachusetts. Archie Butt waited outside on the porch as the two men chatted together. Butt commented to Jimmy Sloan, one of the Secret Service men, that he hoped the meeting would end all the talk about the hostility between the two men. Sloan was not as optimistic. Referring to Roosevelt, he said, "I know this man better than you do. He will come to see the President today and bite his leg off tomorrow."

The Opposition Lines Up

Only a year and a half into the Taft administration and the Republican Party was in total disarray. President Taft had a right to fear that the congressional elections of 1910 would spell more trouble for his administration. Roosevelt, in his home in Oyster Bay, New York, was entertaining Pinchot, La Follette, and James Garfield, leaders of the insurgents and all Taft's sworn enemies. Nellie, reading about Roosevelt's visitors in the newspapers, could only say, "I told you so."

Moreover, Roosevelt had returned to politics with more radical ideas than when he was President. La Follette's and Bryan's ideas had flowed beyond the Midwest and were receiving wide acceptance. Roosevelt, ever politically aware, picked up many of their themes, saying that he stood for a "square deal" between capital and labor and "having those rules changed so as to work for a more substantial equality of opportunity and of reward."

At the same time, the Democratic governor of New Jersey was offering a liberal program that was stirring the nation, a program called the "New Freedom." His name was Woodrow Wilson, and his progressive plan called for an eight-hour work day on public projects, a law against corrupt political practices, and a direct primary for state officers.

Taft, lacking any good public relations label for his program, was unfairly marked as a stagnant conservative, the guardian of the old Cannon-Aldrich regime. Stubbornly courageous and honest about his feelings, Taft refused to bend to those who would have him fire Ballinger or to stop seeing friends like Henry Frick, a director of the United States Steel Corporation, and J. P. Morgan, the multi-millionaire financier. His only concession was to try to meet these people away from public view. One night, he even sneaked past his Secret Service guards in order to play poker at the Frick mansion with his friends.

Despite a superficial show of harmony at the Republican convention in 1910, the election gave the Democrats a majority of 50 in the House and a gain of eight seats in the Senate. The balance of power was now in the hands of the insurgents. Taft's job was going to be harder than ever.

CANADA DEALS A BLOW

In 1911, still smarting from the results of the tariff fight, Taft decided to try a different attack on the trade problem. Rather than trying to get a new tariff bill through Congress, he sought a simple reciprocal United States-Canada trade agreement. There could be no argument that the United States was facing competition from a nation using cheap labor, because the cost of living in both countries was almost identical. The American consumer would benefit from cheaper food imported from Canada, and the United States would gain by greater access to Canada's raw materials. The only opposition would come from East Coast fishermen and Midwest wheat growers in both countries, for these areas were competitive.

This time President Taft fought hard. He sent a special message to the Senate, and he asked various Cabinet members to speak and write on the subject. He made a tiring two-month, 28-state speaking tour, appealing directly to the American people. Sometimes he had to endure shouts of "Hello, Fatty" from discourteous children. When Congress passed the agreement, Taft had a right to be pleased. But his pleasure was short-lived when the Canadian Parliament rejected the agreement.

Sir Wilfred Laurier, the Canadian Prime Minister, had

also championed the agreement. But once again, careless words had the power to destroy good intentions. In a speech to the U.S. House of Representatives, Congressman Champ Clark had said he favored the agreement because "I hope to see the day when an American flag will float over every square foot of the British North American possessions clear to the North Pole." This well-publicized comment fed the fears of Canadians, who saw the agreement as a first step to a takeover of their country by the United States. Clark's remarks made it blatantly clear that such an idea was floating in American heads.

Both Taft and Laurier had put their reputations on the line, and both were defeated. Once again, the press ripped into Taft.

TIME RUNNING OUT

The Sherman Antitrust Act had been passed in 1890. It was the first law written to curb monopolies. Until Roosevelt's administration, the Sherman Act was rarely enforced, and then more against unions than industry. Roosevelt earned a reputation as a "trust-buster" by winning a successful suit against the Northern Securities Company. It earned him praise from the progressives in Congress, and in the seven years of his presidency, he sued a total of 44 major corporations.

Taft's record for four years was 22 suits and 44 indictments. He, too, believed that "combinations to suppress competition or to control prices, and to establish a monopoly are unlawful in so far as they affect interstate trade." As was Taft's way, he would not bend when Republican leaders appealed to him to intervene when a prominent and prosperous Republican was indicted for breaking the Sherman Act. Taft's answer was, "He violated the law and he has to pay the penalty."

But Congress refused to pass legislation that Taft requested which would have strengthened the government's hand in dealing with trusts. Taft's efforts won him few words of praise and earned him the reputation of being antibusiness.

By the time the 1910 congressional elections were over, Taft was well aware that he might not have another four years as President. Little time remained in his first term to accomplish the many things he had hoped to achieve: better relations with countries of Central and South America, a more efficient government, a reduction in the high cost of living, and treaties with countries in Europe and Asia that would improve the possibility of world peace.

It is hard to believe that, up to Taft's time, the country had never had a formal budget or used cost-accounting procedures. Taft was able to get various departments to cut back on staff in order to reduce expenses, but Congress refused to pass legislation that would have created an annual budget.

Dollar Diplomacy

President Taft also failed in his attempts to win friends in Latin America and elsewhere through "dollar diplomacy." This was the belief that promoting trade relations between the United States and another country would be advantageous to both. It would provide employment and higher wages for the foreign nation and a profit for American businessmen willing to take the risk of investing abroad. Unfortunately, Taft, like other Presidents, was forced to send the Navy or the Marines to intervene when American business property was threatened. This only added to the distrust of the United States and the fear of American takeovers.

Mexico was a prime example of failed dollar diplomacy. Taft's visit with President Diaz in 1910 failed to save the Mexican from being ousted from office. By 1911, American troops were mobilized on the nation's southern border to save Diaz's regime and American business investments in Mexico, totaling a billion dollars. But the presence of American troops failed to stem the tide of revolution. Diaz was forced to flee. His elected successor, Francisco Madero, tried to control the bandits and rebels who roamed the countryside. Madero turned out to be a leader of causes but not a competent leader of men. In 1913 Madero was overthrown and assassinated by a disloyal army headed by General Victoriano Huerte shortly before Taft turned over the reins of the United States government to the next President. The Mexican problem was left for the new President to solve.

Chapter 10

The End of a Friendship

The presidential election of 1912 was one of the strangest and most dramatic in American history. It included an attempted assassination, the election-week death of one of the candidates, and three political conventions, one in which there were charges of fraud and another in which more than 40 ballots were needed to select a nominee. When it was over, a friendship was destroyed and the Republican Party split asunder. The actors in the drama were a university president turned governor, a former President turned African hunter, and a man who would have preferred to be sitting on the Supreme Court than to be running for the presidency.

Because he had become President by succession when President McKinley had been assassinated, Theodore Roosevelt could not suppress his joy when, at the end of his first term, he was elected to a second term in a stunning victory. On election night, he impulsively declared to his family and those celebrating with him, "I shall never be a candidate for or accept another nomination." Roosevelt would live to eat those words. Four years later, he would be battling for the presidency with the man he had personally selected and helped to succeed him—William Howard Taft.

THE ROOTS OF THE PROBLEM

What factors forced Teddy Roosevelt to change his mind about his friend, Will Taft, and to decide to run for the presidency himself?

Perhaps initially he was disappointed when Taft, as Roosevelt's personal choice for the presidency, failed to campaign with the kind of enthusiasm that Roosevelt expected in a candidate. Perhaps the former President realized that retiring at age 51 was a big mistake, that he was too young and vigorous to bow out of the political scene at such an early age. Taft, in turn, was upset with Roosevelt's constant contact with the insurgents in the Republican Party.

The headline "ROOSEVELT FOOLED!" was probably the final straw that compelled Roosevelt to run again for the presidency. That headline in all the newspapers around the country resulted from an antitrust suit brought against the United States Steel Corporation in 1911. One of the charges against the company stated that the company's power as a corporate monopoly had been increased when Roosevelt gave permission for U.S. Steel to take over the Tennessee Coal, Iron and Railroad Company during an economic depression called the Panic of 1907.

Though Taft knew about and approved of the suit, he had not had time to learn all the details, because he was about to leave on one of his long railroad trips around the country. He was unaware that Roosevelt would be called to defend himself against the charges, which were that he had been deceived and misled by the directors of the U.S Steel Corporation into approving the merger.

Roosevelt declared that he had not been duped. The Panic of 1907 had created a financial crisis in the nation. Roosevelt insisted that he had taken the action in order to prevent another business failure, to stop the panic, and to restore confidence in the faltering economy. Roosevelt argued that he had approved the merger, but only *after* he had asked for and received the advice of Taft and other members of his Cabinet at that time.

The publicity from the case brought Roosevelt once more to the attention of the country. His vigorous defense won more praise than expected. It encouraged Roosevelt supporters to get back into the political arena. But the case only increased the anti-Taft feelings. The President's pursuit of antitrust actions irritated the conservatives of his party and hurt him politically.

A Tired President Fights On

Nellie Taft had little heart for the 1912 presidential election. She conceded that she did not expect her husband to be re-elected, but she desperately wanted him to beat Roosevelt for the Republican nomination.

Will Taft was tired, obese, and depressed. An artist commissioned to paint his portrait found it an impossible task. "The President is so weary that it shows in his face," the artist said. It was even rumored that Taft had fallen asleep when another artist tried to do a portrait of him.

Taft would have liked nothing better than to retire with honor. But he was now a man with a mission. To Taft, "the whole fate of constitutional government" was at stake. He could not let the nation get into the hands of Roosevelt—a man whose goals seemed to be the destruction of an independent judiciary as well as of representative government.

"I am afraid I am in for a hard fight," Taft said, "but I am going to stay in anyhow. . . . I believe I represent a safer and saner view of our government and its Constitution than

Despite being overweight, Taft enjoyed playing tennis and golf and riding horseback with friends. (Library of Congress.)

Theodore Roosevelt, and whether beaten or not, I mean to continue to labor . . . for those principles."

It was Taft's hope that the election would be fought without personal animosity between two honorable gentlemen. Taft held to this hope as long as he could, but he was soon forced to return Roosevelt's vicious attacks.

However, even when things looked bleak, Taft maintained his sense of humor. He had made 55 speeches in his native state, Ohio, denying the charges that Roosevelt had hurled at him. But when he lost the Ohio primary, he took time to console a supporter. "I do not think you need to be overcome with mortification [humiliation]. After all, you had a pretty heavy candidate to carry."

In February 1912, Roosevelt made his candidacy official with his famous battle cry, "My hat is in the ring." When Taft won the first primaries in New York State, Roosevelt questioned the honesty of the proceedings. He also declared that the only way Taft could win at the Republican National Convention was by "deliberate cheating."

Now Taft began hitting back. He charged Roosevelt with reversing himself on policies he had pushed while he was President. Taft implied that Roosevelt's nomination might bring about a possible dictatorship. If Roosevelt were to seek a third term and the tradition of "only two terms," begun by Washington, was broken, what would prevent Roosevelt from seeking "as many terms as his natural life would permit?" Could one "who has so misunderstood what liberty regulated by law is . . . be entrusted with successive presidential terms?"

The death of Archie Butt in the sinking of the *Titanic* broke another bond between Taft and Roosevelt. Butt had served them both and had been torn by his loyalties as the 1912 campaign heated up. Both candidates mourned his death. Butt was spared the final agony of being a spectator to the terrible insults both men would soon be hurling at one another.

THE REPUBLICAN CONVENTION

The 1912 Republican National Convention was bitter and ugly. It was punctuated by hisses, catcalls, and fistfights. Both major candidates had the backing of corrupt politicians and large sums of money. Taft remained in the White House during the proceedings. Roosevelt was in Chicago that June, marshalling his forces.

The Sinking of the Titanic

The newspaper editions of April 15, 1912, were filled with news from both the Taft and Roosevelt camps. However, the nation's attention was riveted elsewhere, to the tragedy heralded in the headlines. The great British ocean liner, the *Titanic,* had sunk on its maiden voyage. The biggest and most luxurious ship afloat at that time, it was acclaimed as unsinkable. It was said that four of the 16 watertight compartments in its hull could be flooded and it would still remain afloat.

But as it was steaming ahead at full speed in the North Atlantic Ocean off the Grand Banks of Newfoundland, it struck an iceberg just before midnight. The impact ripped through five of the watertight compartments. Within 2½ hours, the huge liner had sunk into the black, still sea, with a loss of 1,513 lives. The passenger list included such prominent names as Astor, Guggenheim, and Major Archie Butt, White House aide to President William Howard Taft.

Butt was returning from a well-deserved vacation abroad. He was playing bridge in a lounge when the collision occurred. The shock seemed so mild that he and the other players did not even stop the game. But before long, the noise and excitement from the boat deck made them aware of the severity of the accident. They soon discovered that the ship was sinking and there were only enough lifeboats for 1,178 of the 2,224 people aboard.

The last moments of Major Butt's life were reported by a former White House associate, Miss Marie Young, who had been a music teacher for the Roosevelt children when Archie Butt was President Roosevelt's aide. In an interview, Miss Young recounted that ''Archie himself put me into the boat, wrapped blankets around me and tucked me in as carefully as if we were starting on a motor ride.'' She remembered that he was very calm, almost oblivious to the fact that his death was just a few minutes away. Then he stepped back, tipped his hat, and said quietly, ''Will you kindly remember me to all the folks back home?''

The terrible loss at sea created so much anger that the first International Convention for Safety of Life at Sea was called in London the following year. One of its findings was that another ocean liner had been only 20 miles away but its radio operator had shut off the equipment for the night. Had the distress signal from the *Titanic* been heard, many more lives might have been saved. Those who were in lifeboats would not have survived the icy sea if they had not been picked up by another British liner, the *Carpathia,* an hour and twenty minutes after the *Titanic* went down.

As a result of the investigation, a set of international rules for ocean safety was created. Among them was a rule that all ships were to have a 24-hour radio watch, routine lifeboat drills, and adequate lifeboat space for every person aboard.

Roosevelt's arrival in Chicago was heralded by huge crowds at the railroad station and at the Congress Hotel. He greeted the crowds wearing his large-brimmed Rough Rider hat, symbol of his days as a hero of the Spanish-American War.

"How do you feel?" yelled a reporter. A grinning Roosevelt shouted back, "I feel like a bull moose." The crowd roared its approval, and the symbol for Roosevelt's soon-to-be third party was born — the bull moose.

Roosevelt had won victories in every state that had primaries except Wisconsin and North Dakota. In those, Robert La Follette had won. After his poor showing elsewhere, La Follette supporters began to flock to the Roosevelt banner. Taft had won delegates in states where the delegates were chosen by the traditional convention method.

The primary system, begun in Wisconsin in 1903, gave voters the opportunity to have a say in the selection of delegates and to commit to whomever they wished at the convention. Roosevelt charged that many of the Taft delegates chosen at the state conventions were not honestly selected. Fraud was a real possibility since the selection of delegates under state election laws tended to be lax and poorly enforced.

According to the Republican Party rules, it was the task of the members of the Republican National Committee to decide which delegates had valid credentials and which did not. The majority of the committee were pro-Taft. They had been chosen at the 1908 convention, in which Roosevelt had played such a leading role. Under the rules approved by Roosevelt at that time, newly elected committee men did not sit on the committee until *after* the convention. If Roosevelt could have the rules changed so that newly elected committee men were seated *before* the delegates were officially seated, he had a good chance of having his charges of fraud decided in his favor.

In the floor battle that ensued, the old guard held firm. A credential committee sympathetic to Taft judged the evidence presented and voted against most of Roosevelt's charges, calling them invalid.

Caught in the middle of the convention furor was Elihu Root, a Cabinet member in both the Roosevelt and Taft administrations. Like Archie Butt, he had also been a friend to both Presidents. Now, as chairman of the convention, Root was forced to uphold the old rules. As keynote speaker, he spoke of the need to defend the Constitution and the courts. It was an unusual keynote speech, for it was directed against Roosevelt rather than the Democratic Party.

On the fifth day of the convention, Warren G. Harding (later to become 29th President of the United States) placed Taft's name in nomination. Chairman Root moved the action along at such a rapid pace that one Roosevelt supporter shouted out, "I make the point that the steamroller is exceeding the speed limit." The steamroller tactics helped Taft win the nomination, and Vice-President Sherman was renominated as well.

The Bull Moose Is Born

Would Roosevelt support the nominee of the Republican convention? Reporters had been asking that question for some time. In February of the election year, Roosevelt had retorted, "Of course, I shall!" But by the time the convention was over, the old Rough Rider had changed his tune.

On the last night of the convention, Roosevelt gathered his supporters in Orchestra Hall and made a speech. It began, "Thou Shalt Not Steal!" Then and there, the Progressive Party, nicknamed by the press "The Bull Moose Party," was born. A party convention was held in August in Chicago, and Roosevelt was proclaimed as the nominee of the new third party.

A THREE-MAN RACE

On viewing the results of the Republican convention, the man who was to become the Democratic candidate, Woodrow Wilson, said, "Good old Teddy. What a help he is." With the split in the Republican Party, chances of a Democratic victory in November skyrocketed.

The Democratic National Convention opened the last week in June. Baltimore, Maryland, the host city, was suffering from a heat wave, and the continuous balloting in the steaming armory no doubt raised the temperature of the delegates. Among those watching the proceedings in the gallery were Mrs. Taft and Alice Roosevelt Longworth, Teddy's daughter. The Democratic race was between Senator Champ Clark, a conservative, and Woodrow Wilson, governor of New Jersey, a progressive.

Woodrow Wilson was a former law professor and president of Princeton University who had been elected governor in 1910. In only two years his progressive ideas had brought him national fame and a possible nomination as the Democratic candidate. Day after day the balloting went on, see-sawing first to Clark, then to Wilson, and back again. The heat continued and tempers flared. At last, on the eighth day, on the 46th ballot, the progressives won. Wilson now headed a shaken party, but not a split one.

Taft was astute enough to know that the Roosevelt and Wilson candidacies meant that the nation was moving in a more liberal and progressive direction. Labeled a conservative, Taft had no illusions that he could win. He had won the battle to wrest the Republican nomination from Roosevelt, but he had no great desire to spend another four years in the White House. From the day of his nomination until election day, he made no speeches except the one accepting his nomination.

Wilson and Roosevelt campaigned ferociously. Roosevelt

The presidential campaign of 1912 was a three-way race. Taft, riding the elephant, was the Republican candidate, Woodrow Wilson is riding the Democratic symbol, the donkey, and Theodore Roosevelt is riding his third-party symbol, the bull moose. This cartoon was a campaign poster for Taft. (Library of Congress.)

made a cross-country tour, attacking both of his opponents wherever he spoke. Wilson, warming up to the growing crowds that greeted him, became more relaxed with his audiences and less like a college professor. He baited Roosevelt by calling the Bull Moose platform a collection of impossible promises. While the newspapers reported daily accounts of speeches and the size of the crowds in the Wilson and Roosevelt campaigns, they could find little to report about Taft except his golf scores.

An Attempted Assassination

On September 21, Roosevelt was in Milwaukee, Wisconsin, preparing to leave his hotel for a speech when a shot rang out. It had been fired by a mentally deranged man who was quickly captured. Though stunned by the bullet, Roosevelt refused to go to the hospital and insisted on being taken to the waiting audience. Speaking before the crowd, he briefly recounted the incident, concluding "It takes more than that to kill a bull moose!" The audience was first shocked and then became so worried about his condition that they could hardly concentrate on his words.

Only when the speech was finished was Roosevelt ready to go to the hospital. Fortunately, the injury was not a severe one. Both Taft and Wilson made the gentlemanly offer of calling off the campaign until Roosevelt was once more ready for the campaign trail, but Roosevelt refused the offer. He knew how well his "plucky image" was working with the voters.

It was Taft who was dealt the final blow of the campaign. On October 30, a week before the election, his running mate, "Sunny Jim" Sherman, died. A substitute, Dr. Nicholas Murray Butler, president of Columbia University in New York City, was quickly added to the ticket. But the last-minute effort was in vain.

Taft returned to Cincinnati to vote. By 10:45 that night, the results were in. Wilson had 436 electoral votes and Roosevelt, 88. Taft had suffered the worst defeat of any President. He received only eight electoral votes, from Vermont and Utah. Taft's only comfort was that hundreds of thousands of Republicans had switched to Wilson in order to save the country from Roosevelt.

A NOT-SO-SAD FAREWELL

"I'll be glad to be going; this is the loneliest place in the world."
Those were Taft's words to the new President, Woodrow Wilson, immediately following the latter's inauguration. There
had been good weather this time, and the Tafts almost seemed
relieved as they finished their good-byes. Despite the disappointment of the last years, Taft could look back with some
satisfaction on the accomplishments of his administration.

He had undertaken the first tariff revision since 1897,
a task even Roosevelt had not dared to tackle. He had put
the conservation program on a legal basis. He had established
the Department of Labor and strengthened the Pure Food and
Drug Act. For the first time, an eight-hour work day was ordered for all federal projects.

Though he had not achieved his goal of establishing a
federal budget, he had raised the issue upon which later administrations would finally act. Taft had also shown that there
could be greater efficiency and economy in government.

The Taft administration witnessed the admission of two
new states to the Union—New Mexico and Arizona—both
in 1912, as well as the addition of two new amendments to
the Constitution. The 16th Amendment gave Congress the
power to collect income taxes. The 17th Amendment ordered
the direct popular vote of senators rather than their selection
by state legislatures.

Perhaps the achievement Taft was most proud of was
his appointments of six excellent men to the Supreme Court,
including the appointment of Charles Evans Hughes as Chief
Justice. Hughes has been rated second only to the first Supreme Court Chief Justice, John Marshall. Taft must have
looked a bit enviously at these men, but he, too, would eventually have his day on that esteemed Court.

Chapter 11

The Dream Comes True

"The truth is, that in my present life, I don't remember that I ever was President." Those words, written by Taft four years after his appointment to the U.S. Supreme Court, express his feelings about his two great roles in life. No other man in American history has ever been head of both the executive and judicial branches of government. For Taft, his dream could only be fulfilled when he was appointed Chief Justice of the Supreme Court. He would need to wait for eight years after his presidency, but those years would be filled with rich experiences, some more rewarding than others.

Following his defeat in the 1912 presidential election, Taft once more regained his zest for life and his sense of humor. He was toying with the not-very-appealing idea of resuming a law practice in his hometown, Cincinnati, when he was offered the position of professor of law at Yale University. Though that meant a move to New Haven, Connecticut, he was delighted with the offer. The idea of teaching his ideas about the Constitution and world peace to a group of bright young people was irresistible.

RETURN TO THE HALLS OF IVY

The eight years Taft spent on the Yale campus were very happy ones. He could take great pride in the success of his children, Helen at Bryn Mawr College; Charlie, making high grades at a prep school run by Uncle Horace Taft; and Robert, receiving high praise for his work at Harvard Law School. (Robert would later serve as Republican leader of the Senate, earning him the nickname of "Mr. Republican." He would also be considered a candidate for the presidency several times, though he would never receive the nomination of his party.)

Though Taft's salary of $5,000 as a college professor hardly matched the $100,000 he received each year for salary and expenses during his presidency, he soon found himself much in demand as a public speaker. For a man who had seemed lethargic at times, more interested in golf and traveling around the country than in the business of the chief executive, Taft now was on a busy, self-imposed, full-time schedule. He was often away from the campus three or four days a week, speaking to a wide variety of groups, from women's organizations and chambers of commerce to civic groups and manufacturers' associations. The income from these engagements provided him with financial security for the rest of his life. He was also much involved in his work with the American Bar Association, having been elected president of that organization in 1913.

Taft's teaching also gave him a great deal of satisfaction once he got the hang of it. Initially, his students seemed enthralled with the novelty of having a former President of the United States as a teacher. But after awhile, some of his more serious students approached him to complain about how boring his classes were. He listened seriously to their concerns and suggestions and changed his presentations.

Taft had been teaching much as he had been taught. In his days at Yale, students would read the textbook assignments they were given as homework and the next day be asked to recite the answers to questions the professor posed. Taft's students asked him to lecture to them, to give them his firsthand experiences as a lawyer and as a President working with Congress. He took their suggestions and began to illustrate the principles of government and law through the use of anecdotes and personal stories. His classes became so popular and enjoyable that students sometimes rose at the end of a lecture to applaud him enthusiastically.

THE PEACEMAKER

Though Taft seemed content with his teaching and speaking engagements, there was no way that he could retire completely from the political arena. Even during his years at Yale, he continued to be involved in the idea of world peace. The concept of a world peace movement began while Taft was President, when he, Secretary of State Philander C. Knox, and Woodrow Wilson endorsed a new organization called the American Society for the Judicial Settlement of International Disputes.

Taft had been successful in the Philippines in reconciling differences between groups. He believed that disagreements between nations could also be reconciled peacefully by arbitration (settling a controversy by hearing both sides and having an impartial judge decide the issue). The peace movement had taken hold in the American public's mind to such an extent that, in 1910, Congress passed a joint resolution calling for the creation of a peace commission.

But when Taft tried to interest the European powers in the idea, he found little support. The only two nations that considered the notion seriously were Great Britain and France. They agreed to sign peace treaties with the United States. The Senate, the agency responsible for approving such agreements, proceeded to alter the treaties on the grounds that they would limit the way foreign affairs could be conducted by the President and the Senate. By the time the amended documents were turned over to Taft, they did little to advance the cause of world peace.

He summed up his disappointment with a humorous poke at himself. "So I put them [the treaties] on the shelf," he said, "and let the dust accumulate on them in the hope that the Senators might change their minds, or that the people might change the Senate; instead of which they changed me" (referring to his loss for re-election).

A Call from the President

Taft's hopes for peace were shattered in 1914, when World War I broke out. Taft agreed with President Wilson's call for strict neutrality on the part of the United States. Neutrality, however, was impossible to maintain. Both the British and the Germans were illegally stopping and searching American ships, and the German submarine fleet in the Atlantic was interrupting American trade. In 1915, a British ocean liner, the *Lusitania,* was torpedoed and sank with a loss of 128 American lives. The American people were outraged, and Wilson tried hard to salvage the situation with diplomatic negotiations. But when three American merchant ships were later sunk by German submarines, Wilson had no alternative but to declare war on April 16, 1917. By September 1918, more than a million Americans were serving in France.

During the war, labor problems created by increases in the cost of living and the reluctance of employers to raise wages compelled Wilson to seek out Taft. Once again his expertise at negotiations was called into play. In 1918 Wilson appointed him as a co-chairman, along with attorney Frank P. Walsh, to head the National War Labor Board. The year Taft spent on that assignment brought him face to face with workers in textile mills and munitions factories.

As Taft visited various manufacturing plants, he gained firsthand knowledge of working conditions. What he saw gave him a new understanding of labor, which would modify his conservative views when he later served on the Supreme Court. The work of the War Labor Board resulted in the adoption of wage standards and maximum hours of employment. The board's work would be cited as a precedent for settling later railroad labor disputes and for the creation of the National Labor Relations Board 15 years later, during the administration of President Franklin D. Roosevelt.

A Second Chance at Peace

The idea of a League of Nations had been bubbling on the surface two years before Wilson publicly committed himself to the idea. Taft had become president of an organization called the *League to Enforce Peace.* The League was based on Taft's concept of international abitration, which he had pushed for when he was President. The major difference in the new plan was that it called for international enforcement, meaning nations in the League would use both military and economic pressure to punish any country that broke the peace.

When Wilson announced his own "Fourteen Points" peace plan in 1918, he included the idea of a general association of nations. In 1919 Wilson went to Paris for peace talks and to present his own concept of a League of Nations. While Wilson was abroad, Taft toured the country in support of Wilson's ideas. As he toured the nation, he noted that women in particular were the strongest advocates of the League and of peace, and he began to have fresh thoughts in favor of giving women the right to vote.

On Wilson's return from Paris, he faced a hostile Republican Senate. Though Wilson had accepted several of Taft's suggestions in his plan for the League, he had failed to include him as a member of the American peace mission to Paris. Wilson also failed to include Elihu Root or other Republican leaders who had the confidence of the public. Rather, Wilson preferred men he could control—members of his own Democratic Party.

Trying to Save the League

After studying the documents that Wilson had brought back from Europe, many senators raised objections on the grounds that the League could become a "superstate" and that the United States could be plunged into war without congressional consent. Wilson, however, refused any suggestions for changing the plan. He would not compromise. He insisted that he would take his case to the people and calmly discuss the provisions of the League document with them.

Quite the opposite occurred. In his passionate defense of the League, Wilson lost control of his tongue, his reputation, and his goal. At meeting after meeting, he hurled one insult after another at his enemies, particularly those in the Senate, the very people whose votes he needed, calling them a "battalion of death." The exhausting tour destroyed Wilson physically and emotionally. In the fall of 1919, in Pueblo, Colorado, Wilson suffered a stroke from which he never recovered.

Taft tried desperately to save the League. "I beg you," he told reluctant senators, "consider the consequences if you defeat the treaty. . . . We are in sight of the promised land. . . Don't prevent our reaching there."

The battle, however, was lost. Twice, the League treaty was voted on in the Senate. Twice it failed to receive a two-thirds majority, as required by the Constitution. Taft blamed Wilson for the loss, never forgiving the President for his uncompromising and stubborn stand. Without the participation of the United States, the weakened League of Nations never achieved its goal of world peace. It would take another 30 years and another world war for the dream to be revived, this time through an organization called the United Nations.

RECONCILIATION WITH ROOSEVELT

After Taft's defeat in 1912, he and Theodore Roosevelt met only twice over the next six years: once when both of them were pallbearers at the funeral of Whitlaw Reed, American ambassador to Great Britain, and once again at a reception for Charles Evans Hughes, Republican candidate for President in 1916. On these occasions, both Taft and Roosevelt had been civil and courteous—but nothing more. A bit later, when Roosevelt was hospitalized, Taft wired a message wishing Roosevelt a speedy recovery. Roosevelt responded with a note of appreciation.

Early in 1918, however, the two former Presidents met by accident while both were staying at the Blackstone Hotel in Chicago. When Taft was told that Roosevelt was dining alone in the dining room, Taft moved as quickly as his large frame would allow. Roosevelt was intent on his meal, but the sudden silence in the room alerted him, and he looked up. There, coming across the room was Taft. Throwing down his napkin, Roosevelt rose and extended his hand. They clapped each other on the back. The diners, who had been watching this dramatic reunion, began to cheer. Both men grinned and bowed to the diners and then sat down for a quiet chat.

That unexpected meeting opened the door to a renewed friendship. It would never be as strong as it had once been, but it allowed for a renewal of correspondence. Two months later, word flashed around the country that Roosevelt's son, Quentin, had been killed in France in an air battle against German planes. Taft immediately wrote a letter of condolence to the distraught father. The death of his son, along with recurring illness, added to the depression Roosevelt was suffering. At one point, Taft urged Roosevelt to run again for governor of New York, but Roosevelt had no heart for it. He died in his sleep of a blood clot five months after his son's death.

Roosevelt's funeral was a private one to which Taft requested and received an invitation. Upon seeing Taft seated several rows back in the church, Roosevelt's son, Captain Archibald Roosevelt, went up to him and insisted, "You're a dear personal friend and must come up further." Afterwards, Taft spoke of Roosevelt to a fellow mourner, saying he "felt grateful that . . . he had some months earlier re-established their long-time friendship." Nellie Taft did not attend the funeral, nor did she ever get word of Taft's last comment about Roosevelt.

CHIEF JUSTICE TAFT

A war-weary nation responded to Warren G. Harding's 1920 campaign theme: "Back to Normalcy." The voters not only put Harding into the White House, they did so with a landslide victory, putting the Republicans back in power in Congress as well.

Taft did not know Harding well, nor was he particularly impressed with the man's talents. But as a former Republican President, it was not surprising for Taft to be invited to the White House for a meeting with Harding in 1921. What did astonish Taft was Harding's open frankness about an appointment to the Supreme Court, especially since there was no current opening on the bench.

Taft had to concede that such an appointment had been the ambition of his life. "But," Taft added, "I will only accept the position of Chief Justice." Since he had been President, he explained, and had appointed three of the men presently on the Court, Taft felt he could not accept any position other than Chief Justice. Furthermore, Justice Louis Brandeis had been the opposition lawyer when the Ballinger case was being tried.

Harding made no commitment that day, for though the current Chief Justice, Edward White, was ill, he was very much alive and had no intention of retiring. Taft remembered an old adage, "The old men of the court seldom die and they never retire." Taft was not overly optimistic that the call would come.

But it did. Taft's dream was realized when White died a natural death a few months later. Harding's nomination of Taft to be Chief Justice of the Supreme Court was confirmed the same day that it was brought before the Senate, with only four dissenting votes.

One Happy Man

Taft was delighted to be living again in Washington in a lovely new home, with an elevator to his third-floor library. Words of praise were pouring in from everywhere. Taft, garbed in his black robe of office, exuded an air of confidence that he had never experienced before. He loved his work and he loved his life. And the pounds which he had begun to shed as soon as he had left the White House continued to drop away.

One of Taft's biographers believed that Taft's weight problem seemed directly related to his degree of happiness. When

In 1921 Taft achieved his dream of becoming Chief Justice of the United States Supreme Court. Taft is seated in the center of this picture of the nine men on the Court. (Library of Congress.)

things were going well and he was content, his weight went down, because he paid attention to it. During his years in the White House, he weighed as much as 350 pounds. As Chief Justice, the scales hovered around 230–250 pounds. A daily three-mile walk gave him exercise and also helped him to control his weight.

Taft was no longer the languorous (sluggish) man who delayed doing his work, put off writing speeches, and stayed up late at social affairs. Now he rose at 5:15 A.M. and worked for two hours at home before departing for the Court. As he walked the three miles to the Capitol, he became a familiar figure to early-rising Washingtonians. The bridge across Rock Creek Park ravine, over which he walked so often, was later named the Taft Bridge.

The Chief Justice attacked the work of the Court with vigor, often bringing home papers to study after dinner. In his role as Chief Justice, Taft was obligated to attend receptions and social events, but now he limited himself to two nights a week in order to conserve his time and energy for his work. "Things are different now," he explained to a friend. "Much of what I think must be kept to myself." Taft knew that, to maintain the kind of impartial judgment needed on the Court, he could no longer publicly expound his views in speeches or in writing. But that did not prevent him from meeting with congressmen, Presidents, and people in high places to press ideas he believed were good for the Court.

Streamlining the Court

For Taft, the first order of business was bringing greater efficiency, order, and dignity to the Court. He was impatient with lawyers who appeared before the Court in slovenly dress. He expected them to wear vests to cover their ties or to tuck the ties in their belts. Jackets were to be buttoned and umbrellas, hats, and other personal items were to be deposited

This picture of Nellie and William Taft was taken in 1924, in their Washington home. The years 1921–1930, when Taft was serving as Chief Justice of the Supreme Court, were among his happiest. (Library of Congress.)

outside the courtroom. Though patient with attorneys who were well prepared, he could strike fear in the hearts of lawyers when he cleared his throat and began a series of questions with, "Sir, what I want to know. . ."

Taft was dismayed with the behavior of several "weak" members of the Court. Some of the justices were elderly and unwilling to carry their share of the case load. They were also unwilling to retire, despite advanced years and illness. On the other hand, there were those justices Taft respected and found to be interesting. One was Justice Oliver Wendell Holmes, who became one of Taft's closest friends. They walked to work together until both were unable to, and then they drove to work together. Though the two men disagreed on many legal and social issues, Taft found Holmes to be witty and charming, though too much under the influence of Justice Louis Brandeis.

Taft had difficulty overcoming his resentment of Brandeis, but he knew that as Chief Justice, he had to bring harmony to the Court if it was to function efficiently. Brandeis, too, wanted the respect of Taft, and in time, Taft did come to have great respect for the younger man's intelligence. Though they differed in their views of economics and society, Taft concluded that Brandeis was "a hard worker. . . and he pulls his weight in the boat."

In the years that followed Taft's appointment, several of the weaker members of the Court died or retired. They were replaced by younger, more vigorous men, appointed by Republican Presidents (with suggestions from Taft), and who were more compatible with Taft's views.

Bringing Order Out of Chaos

No matter how hard the members of the Supreme Court worked, it was impossible to hear all the cases being sent to them. Each year, the number of cases held over for the next session increased. Instead of being a true court of last appeal, the Supreme Court was forced to take any case in which a point of federal law could be raised, no matter how trivial the issue was.

In addition, there were postwar problems over cancelled war contracts, and the new income tax amendment was being tested by a parade of cases. The 18th Amendment, prohibiting the sale of liquor, brought problems of racketeering and enforcement of the law, adding to the work of an already overburdened court. Similar problems were being experienced by judges of the lower courts. Taft was determined to reform the court system to meet the needs of the 20th century.

Taft had spoken about the Court's heavy work load long before he was appointed to serve on the Supreme Court. He was pleased to be asked to appear before the Senate Judiciary Committee to discuss some of the Court's problems and to make recommendations to remedy the situation. Among Taft's suggestions was one which gave the members of the Supreme Court control over which cases merited the Court's consideration. Behind the scenes, Taft used his influence with state bar associations, law school deans, and various civil organizations to get these groups to support what came to be called the "Judges' Bill." As a result of this bill, passed in February 1925, lawyers today have to file a brief, or concise statement, detailing the facts in a case to convince the Court that the case is worth its consideration. This has helped to streamline the work of the Court by reducing the number and kinds of cases it will hear.

A HOME FOR THE SUPREME COURT

From the beginning of its existence, the Supreme Court had been housed in various sections of the Capitol building, being shifted from area to area at the whim of Congress. At one point, Taft complained about the lack of space for the overflowing stacks of records. "The shelves have to be so high that it takes an aeroplane to reach them." Until the final years of his life, Taft lobbied for a new home for the Supreme Court.

The bill appropriating the money for a Supreme Court building was signed in December 1929. Though Taft did not live to see it, his friend, the new Chief Justice, Charles Evans Hughes, said at the laying of the cornerstone, "We are indebted to the late Chief Justice William Howard Taft more than anyone else. . . . This building is the result of his intelligent persistence."

Decisions! Decisions!

As chief justice, Taft persisted in his characteristic manner of trying to reconcile differences. He found that dissenting opinions between justices tended to delay the decisions of the Supreme Court. He worked hard, encouraging Court members to limit dissenting opinions unless the members felt very strongly on the matter. He would often change his vote if there was a majority against his opinion. Yet there were occasions when he, too, felt strongly that the dissenting voice should be heard.

In the most famous case on wiretapping, *Olmstead versus the United States,* the Court received much criticism for its five to four decision. The case involved federal agents who intercepted telephone calls to the headquarters of a liquor smuggling ring. The evidence collected through the wiretapping of the phones resulted in convictions under the National Prohibition Act.

Taft argued for the majority that the 4th Amendment, guaranteeing security against unreasonable searches and seizures, could not be "expanded to include telephone wires leading to the whole world from the defendant's house or office." Justice Brandeis and Holmes were in the minority, arguing that wiretapping was an invasion of privacy. Taft's majority opinion has since been modified in more recent Court decisions.

In Taft's personal opinion, the most important case decided during his time on the Court was that of *Myers versus the United States* (1926). The case dealt with the right of the President (Wilson) to remove a federal official (Frank Myers, a postmaster) from office. The question was whether an 1876 law requiring the Senate to agree on the discharge of federal officials was constitutional.

In Taft's arguments, he recalled that President Andrew Johnson had similar problems when he was impeached after removing Secretary of War Edwin Stanton. Taft deemed the case important because it was a matter of constitutional law and because, as a former President, he felt strongly about any law which placed limits on the powers of the nation's chief executive. The majority opinion, denying the need for senatorial agreement, was written by Taft.

By and large, the Taft Court reflected the Chief Justice's views. He believed in strict adherence to the Constitution. As an example, he did not think that the Volstead Act, dealing with the prohibition of liquor sales, was good legislation, but as long as it was on the books, he believed in strict enforcement of the law. Several of Taft's decisions reflected a new insight into social problems, particularly in the area of labor, and the need for minimum wages and hours of work. Other decisions made during his tenure on the Court led to federal regulations of the stockyard industry and the establishment of a National Labor Relations Board.

A LIFE FULFILLED

Taft took on so much of the burden of writing Court opinions that his health began to suffer. A digestive disorder kept him from attending the funeral of President Wilson in 1924, and a series of heart attacks prevented him from taking a trip to England with Nellie. His summer vacations in Murray Bay, Canada, gave him the peace and serenity which often helped to restore his overworked mind and body. It was at Murray Bay in September 1927 that his beloved family and friends celebrated his 70th birthday. More than 100 people came for the gala occasion, including his children, their spouses, and 10 grandchildren.

Taft had hoped to serve 10 years on the Court and then retire to his home and his books. But two summers after the festivities at Murray Bay, he realized that he could no longer "pull his weight in the boat." He did not want to be one of those men who hang on to their high posts when they are disabled. The death of his beloved half-brother, Charles, in December 1929 was a great emotional strain for Taft. Though already very ill, he insisted on being present to lay a wreath on Charles' grave.

Nellie hoped that a trip to the sunshine and warmth of North Carolina would help her husband. They were there less than a month when Taft insisted that they had to return to Washington. He could barely speak by the time they arrived. The only time he spoke was when Nellie was at his side, and that was only a murmured "Darling."

On February 3, 1930, Taft sent his resignation to the President of the United States, Herbert Hoover. A month later, on March 8, he died in his sleep. Nellie was with him as he lapsed into his last peaceful sleep.

His work was done.

Taft was buried in a simple ceremony at Arlington National Cemetery, the first President to be so honored.

Bibliography

Anderson, Judith Icke. *William Howard Taft: An Intimate History.* New York: W. W. Norton, 1981. Ms. Anderson has delved into the personal relationships in Taft's life which made him the kind of person and President that he was.

Cotton, Edward H. *William Howard Taft: A Character Study.* Boston: The Beacon Press, 1932. A brief book, five chapters long, describing Taft's personality, character, and friendships and giving an overview of his accomplishments and beliefs.

Duffy, Herbert S. *William Howard Taft.* New York: Minton, Balch, 1930. An old but thorough biography with a larger type than seen in most books today.

Kelly, Frank K. *The Fight for the White House: The Story of 1912.* New York: Thomas Y. Crowell, 1961. A lively and dramatic account of the 1912 election, when Taft and Teddy Roosevelt vied with Woodrow Wilson for the presidency.

Myers, Elizabeth P. *William Howard Taft.* Chicago: Reilly and Lee, 1970. A simply written story of Taft's life. The major portion deals with the years leading up to the presidency, though the book also covers both Taft's years as President and Supreme Court Justice.

Pringle, Henry F. *The Life and Times of William Howard Taft.* Hamden, CT: Archon Books, 1964. The most complete history of William Taft, written in two volumes.

Ross, Ishbel. *An American Family: The Tafts—1678 to 1964.* New York: World, 1964. A fascinating history of the Taft family, from its origins in the Massachusetts Bay Colony in the 1670s to William Taft's son, Robert, the senator from Ohio who also sought the presidency. The major portion of the book deals with the life of President Taft.

Taft, Helen Herron. *Recollections of Full Years.* New York: Dodd Mead, 1914. In this recounting of her life, Taft's wife covers their years together through his presidency. There are excellent descriptions of their life in the Philippines and in the White House, along with interesting photographs.

Severn, Bill. *William Howard Taft: The President Who Became Chief Justice.* New York: David McKay, 1970. A well-written biography that makes for easy reading and a good exploration of Taft's life and career.

Index